AUTISM AND COVID-19

AF738122

AUTISM AND COVID-19

Strategies for Supporters to Help Autistics and Their Families

BY

MATTHEW BENNETT
Independent Researcher, Australia

And

EMMA GOODALL
University of Southern Queensland, Australia

LANCASTER PUBLIC LIBRARY
LANCASTER, PA

emerald
PUBLISHING

United Kingdom – North America – Japan – India
Malaysia – China

Emerald Publishing Limited
Howard House, Wagon Lane, Bingley BD16 1WA, UK

First edition 2022

Copyright © 2022 Matthew Bennett and Emma Goodall.
Published under exclusive licence by Emerald Publishing Limited.

Reprints and permissions service
Contact: permissions@emeraldinsight.com

No part of this book may be reproduced, stored in a retrieval system, transmitted in any form or by any means electronic, mechanical, photocopying, recording or otherwise without either the prior written permission of the publisher or a licence permitting restricted copying issued in the UK by The Copyright Licensing Agency and in the USA by The Copyright Clearance Center. Any opinions expressed in the chapters are those of the authors. Whilst Emerald makes every effort to ensure the quality and accuracy of its content, Emerald makes no representation implied or otherwise, as to the chapters' suitability and application and disclaims any warranties, express or implied, to their use.

British Library Cataloguing in Publication Data
A catalogue record for this book is available from the British Library

ISBN: 978-1-80455-034-2 (Print)
ISBN: 978-1-80455-033-5 (Online)
ISBN: 978-1-80455-035-9 (Epub)

ISOQAR certified Management System, awarded to Emerald for adherence to Environmental standard ISO 14001:2004.

ISOQAR
REGISTERED
Certificate Number 1985
ISO 14001

INVESTOR IN PEOPLE

First and foremost, we would like to dedicate this study to all autistics who have either lost their lives or who have experienced serious illness due to COVID-19. We would also like to dedicate this book to the parents of autistic children who have been negatively impacted by the COVID-19 pandemic. Finally, we would like to acknowledge and dedicate this research to those healthcare professionals who are providing medical care and support to autistics and their families during the COVID-19 pandemic.

CONTENTS

ABSTRACT

Background: The first documented case of coronavirus disease (COVID-19), a disease caused by the virus severe acute respiratory syndrome coronavirus 2 (SARS-CoV-2), occurred about 1 December 2019 in Wuhan, China. By late December 2019, a cluster of atypical pneumonia cases emerged in this city. Most of the patients in this cluster had a connection to the Huanan Seafood Market, which suggests that SARS-CoV-2 was zoonotic in origin. On 30 January 2020, the World Health Organization (WHO) declared COVID-19 a 'public health emergency of international concern'. On 11 March 2020, the WHO re-classified the COVID-19 outbreak a global pandemic. This pandemic has undoubtedly had a transformative impact on our society, economy and daily lives. It has also had an impact on autistics and their families.

Objectives: This study has two objectives. First, to present a synthesis of the literature about the impacts of the COVID-19 pandemic from the perspective of autistics and their families and to highlight any gaps in this field of research. Second, to conduct an online survey that will collect the views of autistics or parents raising autistic children about the gaps identified from the synthesis. To achieve these two objectives the following three research questions were posed:

(1) What are the experiences of the COVID-19 pandemic from the perspective of parents raising autistic children?
(2) What impacts has the COVID-19 pandemic had on autistics?
(3) What are the gaps in our understanding about the impact of the COVID-19 pandemic on autistics and their families?

Source and Methods: With the intention of discovering studies that could answer the three research questions, a search of PubMed, using the key terms *autis** AND *COVID**, was conducted on 4 July 2021. This search resulted in the identification of 188 citations. All of these citations were subjected to a *Preferred Reporting Items for Systematic Reviews and Meta-analysis* analysis process. Using this process, 21 studies were identified that were deemed to answer one of the three research questions. From this literature three gaps were discovered, specifically vaccine hesitancy among autistics and parents raising autistic children, the experiences of autistics living with COVID-19 disease and parenting an autistic child during the COVID-19 pandemic. To address these gaps an online survey was developed and distributed on two separate occasions to autistics and their families. During its first distribution it was open for five weeks, from 13 July 2021 to 20 August 2021, and was completed by 32 respondents. During its second distribution it was open for six weeks, from 6 March 2022 to 17 April 2022, and was completed by 34 respondents.

Findings*:* An examination of the retrieved literature and the results from the two online surveys revealed that autistics and their parents have experienced a considerable amount of stress during state-imposed lockdowns and social distancing requirements. The results collected also showed that autistics were generally receptive to receiving a vaccine that can prevent them from developing COVID-19. A follow-up search of the literature indexed on PubMed using the same search permutations as the previous search was conducted on 27 May 2022. This follow-up search confirmed the results collected from the two online surveys.

Conclusions*:* To our knowledge, this is one of the first books about the impacts of the COVID-19 pandemic on autistics and their families. It is also the first study about vaccine hesitancy among autistics and their families, the experiences of autistics living with COVID-19 disease and parenting an autistic child during the COVID-19 pandemic. However, despite these contributions to this emerging and rapidly evolving public health crisis, the results reported in this study should be cautiously adopted since they were based on a small number of participants who all had the ability to access and read an online survey that was published in English.

LIST OF TABLES, IMAGES, AND FIGURES

LIST OF ACRONYMS

AAoM	Autism Alliance of Michigan
ABC	Aberrant Behavior Checklist
ASD	Autism spectrum disorder
COVID-19	Coronavirus disease
GAD-7	Generalised Anxiety Disorder Scale
GPS	Global positioning system
MERS-CoV	Middle East respiratory syndrome
NHS	National Health Service
PHQ-9	Patient Health Questionnaire-9
PRISMA	Preferred Reporting Items for Systematic Reviews and Meta-analysis
RNA	Ribonucleic acid
SARS-CoV	Severe acute respiratory syndrome coronavirus
SARS-CoV-2	Severe acute respiratory syndrome coronavirus 2
TD	Typically developing
USA	United States of America
WHO	World Health Organization

ABOUT THE AUTHORS

Dr Matthew Bennett holds a PhD in Disability Studies from Flinders University, Australia. He has lectured in Disability Studies at Griffith University, Queensland. He has also advised the Australian Government's Autism CRC and has published articles for the *Journal of Autism and Developmental Disorders*. He is actively involved in supporting autistics to achieve their potential in society by disseminating his knowledge about the autism spectrum via lectures, conference presentations and publications.

Dr Emma Goodall is an adjunct research fellow at the University of Southern Queensland, holds a PhD in Education, focused on teaching students on the autism spectrum. She is an executive member of the Australian Society for Autism Research, independent researcher through Healthy Possibilities, a published author and keynote speaker in the areas of autism, sexuality and relationships, education and interoception.

1

INTRODUCTION

1.1 INTRODUCTION

Coronaviruses are a family of enveloped positive-sense single-stranded ribonucleic acid (RNA) viruses that were first discovered during the 1960s. Compared to other RNA viruses, such as the Human Immunodeficiency Virus Type 1 that is between 9,200 to 9,600 nucleotides, coronaviruses have larger genome sizes, ranging from 27 to 34 kilobases (German Advisory Committee Blood, 2016). The name coronavirus is derived from the Latin word 'corona', which means 'crown' or 'halo'. It has been given this name due to its outer appearance (Valencia, 2020) (see Image 1.1).

There are several different types of coronaviruses that are known to cause disease in humans, including Alphacoronaviruses and Betacoronaviruses. It is widely accepted, particularly among those who study coronaviruses, that Alphacoronaviruses and Betacoronaviruses originated from the bat species *Rousettus leschenaultii*. Not all types of coronaviruses, however, can cause serious illness or death. For example, strains 229E and NL63 of Alphacoronaviruses and strains OC43 and NKU1 of Betacoronaviruses often cause mild flu-like symptoms in humans. However, the Middle East respiratory syndrome (MERS-CoV), severe acute respiratory syndrome coronavirus (SARS-CoV) and severe acute respiratory syndrome coronavirus 2 (SARS-CoV-2) commonly cause severe respiratory illnesses in humans (Valencia, 2020).

The cross-species transmission pathways that coronaviruses have traversed to infect humans from animals has been researched. During 2012, for example, MERS-CoV transmitted from a bat to a camel and then to humans while during 2003 SARS-CoV went from a bat to a civet cat and then to humans (Kirtipal et al., 2020). Currently, the transmission pathway that

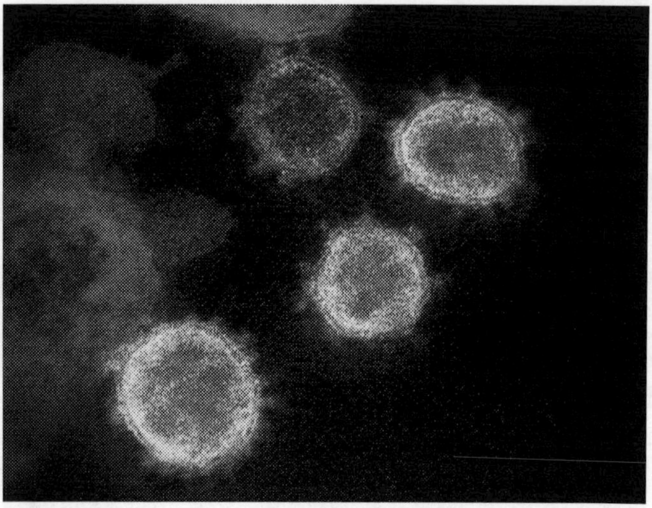

Source: National Institutes of Allergy and Infectious Diseases (2021).

Image 1.1. Image of Severe Acute Respiratory Syndrome Coronavirus 2 (SARS-CoV-2) Virions Taken by the National Institutes of Allergy and Infectious Diseases (NIAID). ***Note*****: Image 1.1 depicts a transmission electron microscope image of the SARS-CoV-2, the virus that causes COVID-19 disease, isolated from a patient in the United States of America. Virus particles are shown emerging from the surface of cells cultured in the lab. The spikes on the outer edge of the virus particles give coronaviruses their name, crown-like. Image captured and colorised at NIAID's Rocky Mountain Laboratories in Hamilton, Montana.**

SARS-CoV-2 took to go from an animal host to humans remains unknown. However, the most plausible transmission pathway appears to be from a bat to a pangolin and then to a human (Hu et al., 2021; Kirtipal et al., 2020; Nadeem et al., 2020; Ye et al., 2020) (see Fig. 1.1).

There are several different ways that SARS-CoV-2 can transmit between humans. As Harrison et al. (2020) illustrate, human-to-human transmission can occur through contact with faecal matter, droplets on surfaces and airborne respiratory droplets. Airborne respiratory transmission is usually most efficient in cold environments, and SARS-CoV-2 can remain on stainless steel and plastic surfaces for up to 72 hours after application (Valencia, 2020) (see Fig. 1.2).

During December 2019 in Wuhan, China, a group of people were diagnosed with atypical pneumonia, with the first known case being diagnosed on 1 December 2019. Most of the patients in this group had a connection to the Huanan Seafood Market, which implies that the then unknown virus had a zoonotic origin. On 30 January 2020, the World Health Organisation (WHO)

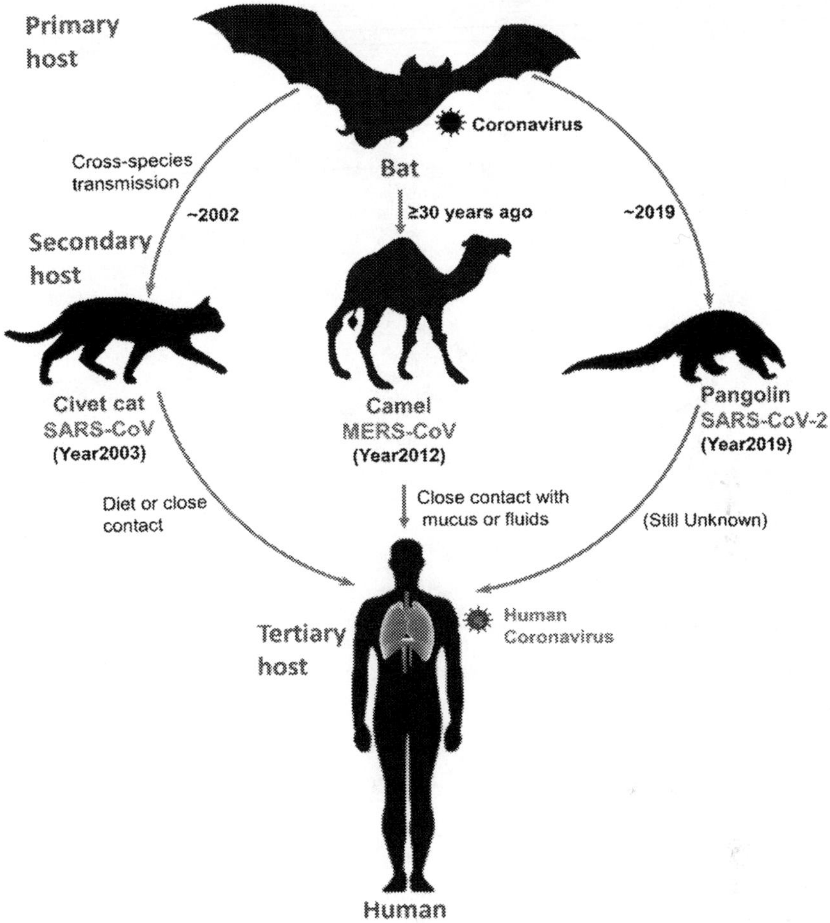

Source: Kirtipal et al. (2020, p. 5).

Fig. 1.1. Cross-Species Transmission Pathways for Three Coronavirus Virions.

declared this medical event a 'public health emergency of international concern'. The WHO then re-classified this event as a global pandemic on 11 March 2020. Prior to its naming, SARS-CoV-2 was called the '2019 novel coronavirus'. To avoid any confusion with regards to SARS-CoV, which was first identified in 2002, it was suggested that it should be called 'human coronavirus 2019'. However, the final and official name of the newly discovered virus was SARS-CoV-2 (Valencia, 2020; Yan et al., 2020).

People who are infected with SARS-CoV-2 and who exhibit symptoms are diagnosed with coronavirus disease (COVID-19). Symptoms can vary between

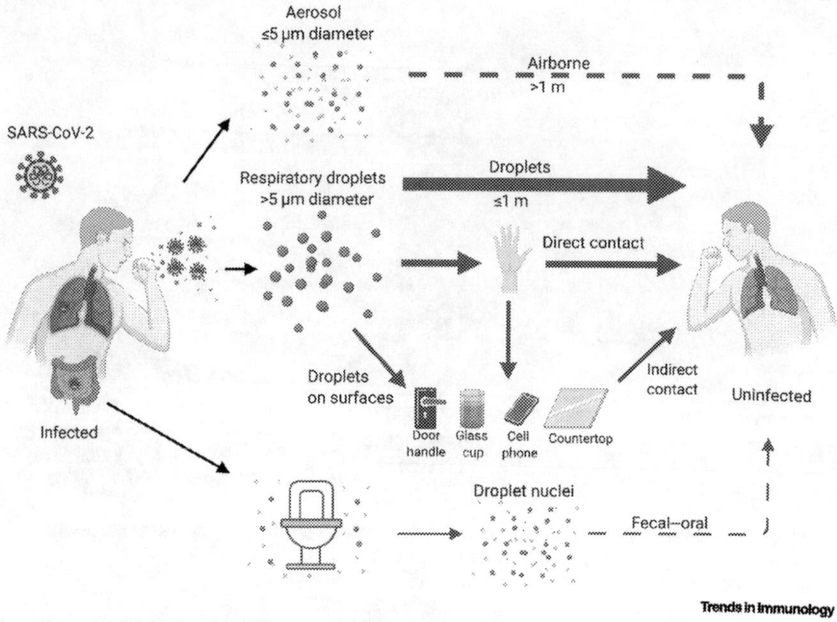

Source: Harrison et al. (2020, p. 1104).

Fig. 1.2. Transmission Pathways for Severe Acute Respiratory Syndrome Coronavirus 2 (SARS-CoV-2).

people, but the main symptoms include fever, chills and a dry cough, sputum production, fatigue, lethargy, arthralgias, myalgias, headache, dyspnoea, nausea, vomiting, anorexia and diarrhoea (Harrison et al., 2020) (see Fig. 1.3). Once infected some individuals may be asymptomatic whilst others will experience either acute respiratory distress syndrome or death. Advanced age and pre-existing chronic medical conditions can increase the severity of a person's COVID-19 symptoms. After infection, the incubation period for SARS-CoV-2 is typically 5.2 days with 97.5% of those infected with this virus developing symptoms within 11.5 days (Valencia, 2020).

During late 2020, different countries approved vaccines that can prevent people developing serious COVID-19 disease after contracting SARS-CoV-2. Pfizer/BioNTech, Moderna, Sputnik V and Oxford–AstraZeneca are common vaccines that have been approved for usage. Doroftei et al.'s (2021) mini-review of 11 studies about the efficiency of COVID-19 vaccines showed that Pfizer/BioNTech (~95%), Moderna (~94%) and Sputnik V (~92%) had an efficacy rate of >90% while Oxford/AstraZeneca had a lower efficacy rate (~81%). Additionally, they could not evaluate the efficacy of Convidicea (AD5-nCOV),

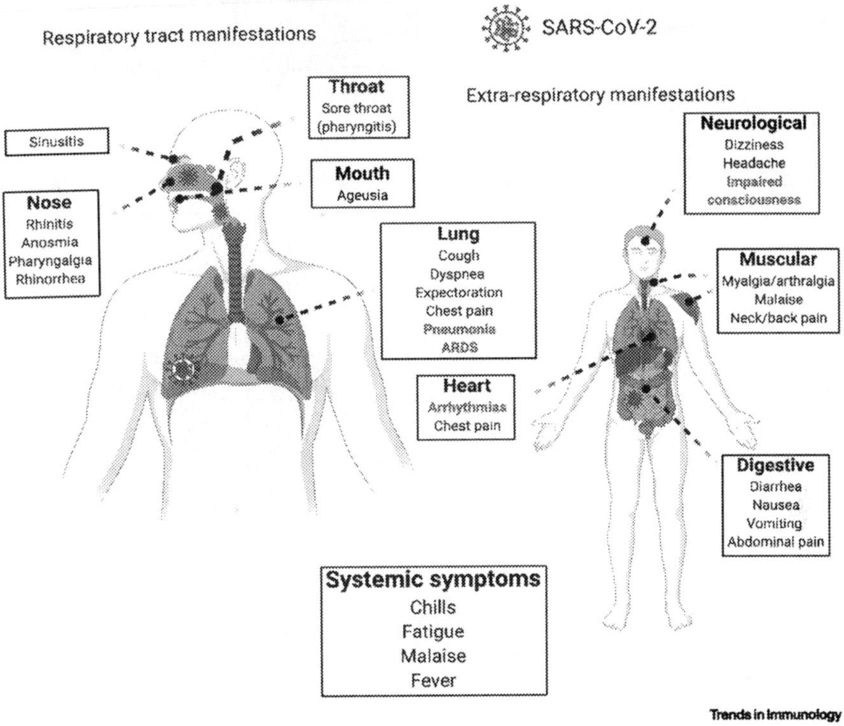

Source: Harrison et al. (2020, p. 1105).

Fig. 1.3. Common Symptoms of COVID-19 Disease.

Johnson & Johnson (Ad26.COV2.S), Sinopharm (BBIBP-CorV), Covaxin (BBV152), and Sinovac (CoronaVac).

The COVID-19 pandemic has caused an unexpected and unprecedented disruption to our society and economy. With the widespread requirement to wear masks and practice social distancing, the ways that we perform our daily activities have profoundly changed. There has been widespread debate and discussion, especially within policy and academic spheres, about the social and economic impacts of the COVID-19 pandemic on the public. However, since the combination of COVID-19 and autism research is a niche field, not much literature about the impacts of this pandemic on autistics and their families has been published. To our knowledge, this book is either the first or one of the first to present a synthesis of peer-reviewed academic literature about some of the known impacts of the COVID-19 pandemic on autistics and their families. It is also arguably one of the first to summarise the gaps in our understanding about this topic and to then present new insights about this once-in-a-century public health crisis.

1.2 THE INTENDED AUDIENCE FOR THIS BOOK

1.2.1 Autistic Adults

There are three reasons why this research is of benefit to autistics. First, autistics will learn what they can expect during the continuing COVID-19 pandemic, especially after reading section '3.3 – What impacts has the COVID-19 pandemic had on autistics?' Equipped with this information they may be able to encounter this pandemic more confidently knowing that their experiences are common for other autistics. Second, this book can be a 'springboard' that can help autistics find additional information about the COVID-19 pandemic. Third, autistic and non-autistic parents can acquire an understanding about what they might encounter during the COVID-19 pandemic, especially after reading section '3.2 – What are the experiences of the COVID-19 pandemic from the perspective of parents raising autistic children?'

1.2.2 Professionals Who Support Autistics

Medical professionals have repeatedly expressed their concerns about the difficulties they confront when supporting autistic patients (Adams & Young, 2020; Calleja et al., 2020; Malik-Soni et al., 2022; Mason et al., 2019; Muskat et al., 2015; Nicolaidis et al., 2015; Raymaker et al., 2017; Unigwe et al., 2017). Adams and Young (2020) reviewed 12 studies about the barriers and enablers that autistics have experienced when they were trying to access psychological treatments. The most cited barrier was a lack of knowledge or unwillingness on behalf of the therapist to tailor their approaches to the autistic client. These results were also echoed by Nicolaidis et al. (2015), who reported that providers' lack of knowledge about autistic adults as well as incorrect assumptions about autistic patients prevented autistics from obtaining effective medical care. It is plausible to assume that since medical professionals have difficulties assisting autistics, they would also have difficulties assisting them during the COVID-19 pandemic. After reading this book, medical professionals should be able to develop an understanding of some of the challenges that autistics are experiencing during the COVID-19 pandemic. They will also learn about some of the challenges that the families of autistic children are encountering during this pandemic. Armed with this information, medical professionals should be able to tailor their approaches to provide more effective support.

1.2.3 Students and Scholars Who Study the Autism Spectrum

Those attending higher education institutions would find this book a valuable source of information. Its contents can help students studying medicine, psychology or social work develop an understanding about some of the challenges that autistics are encountering during the ongoing COVID-19 pandemic. These and other students could also learn about some of the challenges that parents raising autistic children are encountering during this pandemic. For academics, this book can provide them with two benefits. First, they can use its contents to teach their students about the impacts of the ongoing COVID-19 pandemic on autistics. Second, academics can cite the gaps in this field of research, which are outlined in chapter three, in their research activities and grant applications.

REFERENCES

Adams, D., & Young, K. (2020). A systematic review of the perceived barriers and facilitators to accessing psychological treatment for mental health problems in individuals on the autism spectrum. *Review Journal of Autism and Developmental Disorders*, *8*(4), 436–453. https://doi.org/10.1007/s40489-020-00226-7

Calleja, S., Islam, F. M. A., Kingsley, J., & McDonald, R. (2020). Healthcare access for autistic adults: A systematic review. *Medicine*, *99*(29), e20899. https://doi.org/10.1097/MD.0000000000020899

Doroftei, B., Ciobica, A., Ilie, O. D., Maftei, R., & Ilea, C. (2021). Mini-review discussing the reliability and efficiency of COVID-19 vaccines. *Diagnostics (Basel, Switzerland)*, *11*(4), 579. https://doi.org/10.3390/diagnostics11040579

German Advisory Committee Blood (Arbeitskreis Blut), Subgroup 'Assessment of Pathogens Transmissible by Blood'. (2016). Human immunodeficiency virus (HIV). *Transfusion Medicine and Hemotherapy: offizielles Organ der Deutschen Gesellschaft fur Transfusionsmedizin und Immunhamatologie*, *43*(3), 203–222. https://doi.org/10.1159/000445852

Harrison, A. G., Lin, T., & Wang, P. (2020). Mechanisms of SARS-CoV-2 transmission and pathogenesis. *Trends in Immunology*, *41*(12), 1100–1115. https://doi.org/10.1016/j.it.2020.10.004

Hu, B., Guo, H., Zhou, P., & Shi, Z. L. (2021). Characteristics of SARS-CoV-2 and COVID-19. *Nature Reviews Microbiology*, *19*(3), 141–154. https://doi.org/10.1038/s41579-020-00459-7

Kirtipal, N., Bharadwaj, S., & Kang, S. G. (2020). From SARS to SARS-CoV-2, insights on structure, pathogenicity and immunity aspects of pandemic human coronaviruses. *Infection, Genetics and Evolution: Journal of Molecular Epidemiology and Evolutionary Genetics in Infectious Diseases*, *85*, 104502. https://doi.org/10.1016/j.meegid.2020.104502

Malik-Soni, N., Shaker, A., Luck, H., Mullin, A. E., Wiley, R. E., Lewis, M., Fuentes, J., & Frazier, T. W. (2022). Tackling healthcare access barriers for individuals with autism from diagnosis to adulthood. *Pediatric Research*, *91*(5), 1028–1035. https://doi.org/10.1038/s41390-021-01465-y

Mason, D., Ingham, B., Urbanowicz, A., Michael, C., Birtles, H., Woodbury-Smith, M., Brown, T., James, I., Scarlett, C., Nicolaidis, C., & Parr, J. R. (2019). A systematic review of what barriers and facilitators prevent and enable physical healthcare services access for autistic adults. *Journal of Autism and Developmental Disorders*, *49*(8), 3387–3400. https://doi.org/10.1007/s10803-019-04049-2

Muskat, B., Burnham Riosa, P., Nicholas, D. B., Roberts, W., Stoddart, K. P., & Zwaigenbaum, L. (2015). Autism comes to the hospital: The experiences of patients with autism spectrum disorder, their parents and health-care providers at two Canadian paediatric hospitals. *Autism: The International Journal of Research and Practice*, *19*(4), 482–490. https://doi.org/10.1177/1362361314531341

Nadeem, M. S., Zamzami, M. A., Choudhry, H., Murtaza, B. N., Kazmi, I., Ahmad, H., & Shakoori, A. R. (2020). Origin, potential therapeutic targets and treatment for coronavirus disease (COVID-19). *Pathogens (Basel, Switzerland)*, *9*(4), 307. https://doi.org/10.3390/pathogens9040307

National Institutes of Allergy and Infectious Diseases. (2021). New images of novel coronavirus SARS-CoV-2 now available. https://www.niaid.nih.gov/news-events/novel-coronavirus-sarscov2-images

Nicolaidis, C., Raymaker, D. M., Ashkenazy, E., McDonald, K. E., Dern, S., Baggs, A. E., Kapp, S. K., Weiner, M., & Boisclair, W. C. (2015). "Respect the way I need to communicate with you": Healthcare experiences of adults on the autism spectrum. *Autism: The International Journal of Research and Practice*, *19*(7), 824–831. https://doi.org/10.1177/1362361315576221

Raymaker, D. M., McDonald, K. E., Ashkenazy, E., Gerrity, M., Baggs, A. M., Kripke, C., Hourston, S., & Nicolaidis, C. (2017). Barriers to healthcare: Instrument development and comparison between autistic adults and adults with and without other disabilities. *Autism: The International Journal of Research and Practice*, *21*(8), 972–984. https://doi.org/10.1177/1362361316661261

Unigwe, S., Buckley, C., Crane, L., Kenny, L., Remington, A., & Pellicano, E. (2017). GPs' confidence in caring for their patients on the autism spectrum: An online self-report study. *British Journal of General Practice*, *67*(659), e445–e452. https://doi.org/10.3399/bjgp17X690449

Valencia, D. N. (2020). Brief review on COVID-19: The 2020 pandemic caused by SARS-CoV-2. *Cureus*, *12*(3), e7386. https://doi.org/10.7759/cureus.7386

Yan, Y., Shin, W. I., Pang, Y. X., Meng, Y., Lai, J., You, C., & Pang, C. H. (2020). The first 75 Days of novel coronavirus (SARS-CoV-2) outbreak: Recent advances, prevention, and treatment. *International Journal of Environmental Research and Public Health*, *17*(7), 2323. https://doi.org/10.3390/ijerph17072323

Ye, Z. W., Yuan, S., Yuen, K. S., Fung, S. Y., Chan, C. P., & Jin, D. Y. (2020). Zoonotic origins of human coronaviruses. *International Journal of Biological Sciences*, *16*(10), 1686–1697. https://doi.org/10.7150/ijbs.45472

2

METHODOLOGY

2.1 INTRODUCTION

The main objective of this chapter is to outline the steps and rationale for conducting the scoping review that identified the gaps in the research that aided in the development of the online survey. It begins with a brief description of scoping reviews. Arksey and O'Malley's (2005) six steps for creating a scoping review are then outlined as they were used as a guide to create this scoping review. Some of the methodological strengths and weaknesses of this study are then outlined.

Keywords: Preferred reporting items for systematic reviews; meta-analysis (PRISMA) analysis process; PubMed; scoping reviews; selection bias

2.2 AN EXPLANATION OF SCOPING REVIEWS

There are many different analytical approaches that researchers can use to examine the evidence of a topic, such as Bayesian meta-analysis, content analysis or critical interpretative synthesis (Kastner et al., 2012). For this study, a scoping review methodology was used since it was anticipated that there would be a diverse range of studies about the COVID-19 pandemic and autism. Scoping reviews give researchers the opportunity to examine a large amount of diverse research. In contrast, systematic literature reviews only give researchers the flexibility to examine a relatively small number of studies that answer specific research questions (Munn et al., 2018).

Despite their popularity, a definition about scoping reviews and an outline of the steps required to conduct such a review remain elusive (Levac et al.,

2010). However, Arksey and O'Malley's (2005) six-step process for conducting a scoping review is one of the most widely used methods for conducting such a review (see Table 2.1) (Levac et al., 2010). Thus, their process has been used in this study.

Table 2.1. Overview of the Arksey and O'Malley's Six-Step Methodological Framework for Conducting a Scoping Review.

Arksey and O'Malley Framework Stage	Description
Step 1: Identifying the research question	Identifying the research question provides the roadmap for subsequent stages. Relevant aspects of the question must be clearly defined as they have ramifications for search strategies. Research questions are broad in nature as they seek to provide breadth of coverage.
Step 2: Identifying relevant studies	This stage involves identifying the relevant studies and developing a decision plan for where to search, which terms to use, which sources are to be searched, time span and language. Comprehensiveness and breadth is important in the search. Sources include electronic databases, reference lists, hand searching of key journals, and organisations and conferences. Breadth is important; however, practicalities of the search are important as well. Time, budget and personnel resources are potential limiting factors, and decisions need to be made upfront about how these will impact the search.
Step 3: Study selection	Study selection involves post hoc inclusion and exclusion criteria. These criteria are based on the specifics of the research question and on new familiarity with the subject matter through reading the studies.
Step 4: Charting the data	A data-charting form is developed and used to extract data from each study. A 'narrative review' or 'descriptive analytical' method is used to extract contextual or process-oriented information from each study.

Table 2.1. *(Continued)*

Arksey and O'Malley Framework Stage	Description
Step 5: Collating, summarising and reporting results	An analytic framework or thematic construction is used to provide an overview of the breadth of the literature but not a synthesis. A numerical analysis of the extent and nature of studies using tables and charts is presented. A thematic analysis is then presented. Clarity and consistency are required when reporting results.
Step 6: Consultation (optional)	Provides opportunities for consumer and stakeholder involvement to suggest additional references and provide insights beyond those in the literature.

Source: Levac et al. (2010, p. 3).

2.3 SIX-STEP PROCESS USED IN THIS SCOPING REVIEW

2.3.1 Formulating the Research Questions

The first step in Arksey and O'Malley's (2005) approach involves formulating several research questions that can help bring into focus the overarching objective of the study. The objective of this study was to summarise our accumulated knowledge about the consequences of the ongoing COVID-19 pandemic on autistics and their families. The following three research questions were formulated to help achieve this goal:

(1) What are the experiences of the COVID-19 pandemic from the perspective of parents raising autistic children?

(2) What impacts has the COVID-19 pandemic had on autistics?

(3) What are the gaps in our understanding about the impact of the COVID-19 pandemic on autistics and their families?

2.3.2 Identifying Relevant Studies

The second step in Arksey and O'Malley's six-step scoping review process involves developing and then using a plan to search for relevant studies. Often this plan includes an outline of what academic databases will be searched (e.g. SpringerLink., SAGE, PubMed), what terms will be used to retrieve relevant studies from the academic databases, and the inclusion and exclusion criteria that are applied to the studies retrieved. When developing this plan, researchers need to consider all time, budget and personal constraints that may inhibit their ability to locate studies.

For this study, it was decided that a search within PubMed for relevant citations was appropriate. The rationale for this decision was that PubMed typically contains medical literature, including research about the autism spectrum and the COVID-19 pandemic. During 4 July 2021, a search of PubMed was conducted using the search terms 'autis*' AND 'COVID*'. The use of the asterisk (*) allowed a broad combination of terms to be included in the search. For instance, 'autis*' allowed the terms 'autism', 'autism spectrum disorder', 'autism spectrum condition' and 'autistic' to be included. Additionally, due to the large volume of research being produced about the COVID-19 pandemic these search terms were restricted to the article's title and/or abstract (i.e. (autis*[Title/Abstract]) AND (covid*[Title/Abstract])). To ensure the studies retrieved addressed the research questions, a series of inclusion and exclusion criteria were formulated (see Tables 2.2 and 2.3).

Table 2.2. Inclusion Criteria.

Inclusion Criteria	Examples of References
Studies with samples of only autistic participants	Adams et al. (2021), Bal et al. (2021)
Studies with samples of parents raising autistic children	Alhuzimi (2021), Althiabi (2021), Manning et al. (2021)

Table 2.3. Exclusion Criteria.

Exclusion Criteria	Examples of References
Opinion piece, commentary or letter to the editor	Ameis et al. (2020), Cox et al. (2020), Kawabe et al. (2020), Narzisi (2020), Wang (2020)
Did not contain a sample of autistics, their parents or medical professionals who have helped autistics	Dursun et al. (2021), Tarbox et al. (2020)
Case studies of autistics*	Pascariello et al. (2020)
Article in a language other than English (e.g. Spanish, Dutch, French)	Amorim et al. (2020), Cohen (2020), Daaboul et al. (2021)
Article did not mention COVID-19	Hjorth et al. (2019)
Samples contain participants with mixed disabilities	Adamou et al. (2021), Chafouleas and Iovino (2021)
Study did not focus on autism	Tamouza et al. (2021)
Article did not focus on COVID-19	Morris et al. (2021)
Studies in which healthcare professionals have helped autistics	Sheehan et al. (2021), Wagner et al. (2022)

Key: *Case studies were excluded because it was not possible to generalise their findings to the entire autistic community.

2.3.3 Study Selection

The third step in Arksey and O'Malley's approach to creating a scoping review involves selecting relevant studies that can be used to answer the research questions. There are several different techniques that a researcher can use to examine the studies retrieved after searching a database. For example, studies that are deemed to be of interest could be included in the scoping review and then their reference lists could be examined to include additional studies (i.e. a snowballing approach). Since there were 188 citations retrieved from the PubMed search, it would have been a herculean task to use a snowball approach. Thus, the *Preferred Reporting Items for Systematic Reviews and Meta-Analyses* (PRISMA) analysis process was used to examine the citations retrieved.

The PRISMA analysis process is an established method for extracting from many retrieved citations any relevant studies that answer research questions. This analysis process has been used to examine many different topics in the field of autism research, including autistic patients in secure psychiatric care (Allely, 2018). Drawing from such studies, the PRISMA analysis process was used in this scoping review (see Table 2.4, Fig. 2.1).

Table 2.4. The Preferred Reporting Items for Systematic Reviews and Meta-Analyses (PRISMA) Analysis Process in This Study.

Step	Description of the Step
1	The first step in the PRISMA analysis process was to search PubMed for studies about COVID-19 and the autism spectrum.
2	The second step in the PRISMA analysis process involved removing any duplicate records from the PubMed search. It was discovered that no records were duplicates, which resulted in 188 original citations.
3	The third step in the PRISMA analysis process involved reading each study's title and abstract to determine if it met this study's eligibility criteria and answered any of the four guiding research questions. Of the 188 studies that were examined 135 were excluded.
4	The fourth step of the PRISMA analysis process involved reading the entire text of the 53 studies that were judged to be of interest from the previous step. This full-text examination resulted in 32 studies being excluded and 21 studies that were deemed to answer one of this scoping review's four guiding research questions.
5	The fifth step of the PRISMA analysis process involved cataloguing the 21 studies retained from the fourth step that can help address the four guiding research questions.

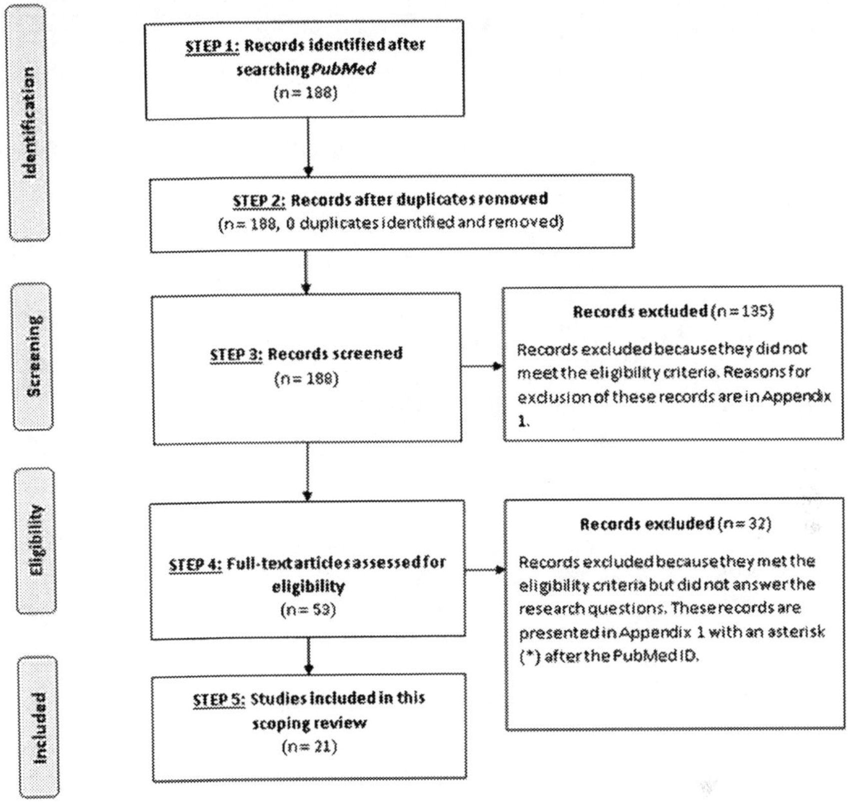

Source: Moher et al. (2009).

Fig. 2.1. Results from the Preferred Reporting Items for Systematic Reviews and Meta-Analysis (PRISMA) Analysis Process.

2.3.4 Charting the Data

The fourth step in Arksey and O'Malley's approach to producing a scoping review involves extracting data from the studies that were deemed to answer one or more of the scoping review's research questions. Basic statistical information about the study was examined, including its publication year along with the number and age range of the participants. By cataloguing these data, it was possible to quickly and efficiently compile, summarise and then report all the data that were identified.

2.3.5 Collating, Summarising and Reporting the Results

The fifth step in Arksey and O'Malley's six-step process to creating a scoping review involves collating, summarising and then reporting all the data that were recorded during the previous process. This information is reported in the next chapter.

2.3.6 Disseminating the Results of the Scoping Review

The sixth and final step in Arksey and O'Malley's outline for producing a scoping review involves presenting the scoping review's results to external stakeholders. This step typically occurs through conference presentations and, in this case, a book.

2.4 METHODOLOGICAL STRENGTHS OF THIS SCOPING REVIEW

2.4.1 Datasets Have Been Published in the Appendices

For a study's findings to be considered truthful, other studies that use the same analysis process and dataset must produce identical findings. Researchers in medicine and psychology have often struggled to validate the truthfulness of their findings because they cannot reproduce such findings using the same dataset and analytical procedures (Johnson et al., 2020; Okanya et al., 2020). This inability has been termed the 'reproducibility crisis'. There are many different factors that have contributed to this crisis. However, one of the most widely accepted and acknowledged causes of this crisis is not providing a study's dataset, either deliberately or unintentionally (Miyakawa, 2020). In the interests of reducing the possibility of this study succumbing to this crisis Appendix 1 lists all the records retrieved from the two searches of PubMed; one search that was conducted before the first online survey was distributed to autistics and their families (i.e. 4 July 2021) and the other conducted after the second online survey sent to autistics and their families closed (i.e. 27 May 2022). In conjunction with this dataset are justifications for why each retrieved citation from PubMed was either included or excluded from this study. Equipped with this information, researchers will be able to either confirm or challenge the results and conclusions reported in this study by repeating the analysis process that was used.

2.4.2 PubMed Search

PubMed was the only database of academic studies searched because it contained more than 30 million records. It was also searched because it listed studies that were published by several reputable academic journals about the autism spectrum, including the *Journal of Autism and Developmental Disorders*, *Autism: The International Journal of Research and Practice*, *Research in Autism Spectrum Disorders* and *Review Journal of Autism and Developmental Disorders*. Due to its coverage, it was decided that searching PubMed was a more comprehensive and efficient approach than conducting individual searches of reputable academic publishers or academic journals.

2.4.3 General Search Terms

Due to the novelty of the COVID-19 pandemic no caveats were placed on the study's publication year or the age of the autistic participants in the study. Removing these caveats ensured that the largest and most diverse range of citations could be retrieved from the PubMed search.

2.5 METHODOLOGICAL LIMITATIONS OF THIS SCOPING REVIEW

2.5.1 Only English Language Studies Were Examined

Only English language studies were examined because both authors were fluent in English. Consequently, non-English studies were not examined. It is possible that non-English studies might have contained insights that would have either contradicted or supported the results reported in this study.

2.5.2 Not Using More Search Terms

The studies examined for this research were all sourced from PubMed. Thus, studies not indexed in PubMed were not collected and examined. In the future, other academic databases should be searched in conjunction with PubMed to ensure that the greatest number of citations would be retrieved for analysis.

Such an approach has yielded a broad range of citations for other research projects (Bramer et al., 2017; Justesen et al., 2021).

2.5.3 Lack of Consultation with Autistics

Another drawback of this study was that autistics were not consulted about its development. If they were consulted, then their insights might have created a more complex understanding of the topic. However, the authors are themselves autistic researchers so there is a level of autistic involvement. Regardless of this drawback, the three research questions did help uncover new discoveries.

2.6 CONCLUSION

This chapter provided the reader with an overview of the steps and rationale for conducting a scoping review. It started with a brief description of scoping reviews, followed by an explanation of the six steps outlined by Arksey and O'Malley for conducting such a review. Some of the methodological strengths and weaknesses of conducting this scoping review were then outlined. The results of this scoping review are presented in the next chapter. These results should help contextualise the gaps in our knowledge about the autism spectrum and the COVID-19 pandemic that the online survey aimed to address.

REFERENCES

Adamou, M., Jones, S. L., Fullen, T., Galab, N., Abbott, K., & Yasmeen, S. (2021). Remote assessment in adults with autism or ADHD: A service user satisfaction survey. *PLoS One*, *16*(3), e0249237. https://doi.org/10.1371/journal.pone.0249237

Adams, R. E., Zheng, S., Taylor, J. L., & Bishop, S. L. (2021). Ten weeks in: COVID-19-related distress in adults with autism spectrum disorder. *Autism: The International Journal of Research and Practice*, *25*(7), 2140–2145. https://doi.org/10.1177/13623613211005919

Alhuzimi, T. (2021). Stress and emotional wellbeing of parents due to change in routine for children with Autism Spectrum Disorder (ASD) at home during COVID-19 pandemic in Saudi Arabia. *Research in Developmental Disabilities*, *108*, 103822. https://doi.org/10.1016/j.ridd.2020.103822

Allely, C. S. (2018). A systematic PRISMA review of individuals with autism spectrum disorder in secure psychiatric care: Prevalence, treatment, risk assessment and other clinical considerations. *Journal of Criminal Psychology*, *8*(1), 58–79. https://doi.org/10.1108/JCP-06-2017-0028

Althiabi, Y. (2021). Attitude, anxiety and perceived mental health care needs among parents of children with Autism Spectrum Disorder (ASD) in Saudi Arabia during COVID-19 pandemic. *Research in Developmental Disabilities*, *111*, 103873. https://doi.org/10.1016/j.ridd.2021.103873

Ameis, S. H., Lai, M. C., Mulsant, B. H., & Szatmari, P. (2020). Coping, fostering resilience, and driving care innovation for autistic people and their families during the COVID-19 pandemic and beyond. *Molecular Autism*, *11*(1), 61. https://doi.org/10.1186/s13229-020-00365-y

Amorim, R., Catarino, S., Miragaia, P., Ferreras, C., Viana, V., & Guardiano, M. (2020). The impact of COVID-19 on children with autism spectrum disorder [Impacto de la COVID-19 en niños con trastorno del espectro autista]. *Revista de Neurologia*, *71*(8), 285–291. https://doi.org/10.33588/rn.7108.2020381

Arksey, H., & O'Malley, L. (2005). Scoping studies: Towards a methodological framework. *International Journal of Social Research Methodology*, *8*(1), 19–32. https://doi.org/10.1080/1364557032000119616

Bal, V. H., Wilkinson, E., White, L. C., Law, J. K., SPARK Consortium, Feliciano, P., & Chung, W. K. (2021). Early pandemic experiences of autistic adults: Predictors of psychological distress. *Autism Research: Official Journal of the International Society for Autism Research*, *14*(6), 1209–1219. https://doi.org/10.1002/aur.2480

Bramer, W. M., Rethlefsen, M. L., Kleijnen, J., & Franco, O. H. (2017). Optimal database combinations for literature searches in systematic reviews: A prospective exploratory study. *Systematic Reviews*, *6*(1), 245. https://doi.org/10.1186/s13643-017-0644-y

Chafouleas, S. M., & Iovino, E. A. (2021). Comparing the initial impact of COVID-19 on burden and psychological distress among family caregivers of children with and without developmental disabilities. *School*

Psychology (Washington, DC), *36*(5), 358–366. https://doi.org/10.1037/spq0000426

Cohen, D. (2020). Appréhender le COVID-19 au fil de l'eau en tant que psychiatre d'enfant et d'adolescent [Appreciating COVID-19 as a child and adolescent psychiatrist on the move]. *L'Encephale*, *46*(3S), S99–S106. https://doi.org/10.1016/j.encep.2020.05.005

Cox, D. J., Plavnick, J. B., & Brodhead, M. T. (2020). A proposed process for risk mitigation during the COVID-19 pandemic. *Behavior Analysis in Practice*, *13*(2), 299–305. https://doi.org/10.1007/s40617-020-00430-1

Daaboul, J., Tamouza, R., & Leboyer, M. (2021). Immuno-psychiatrie et pandémie de SARS-CoV-2 : Liens et possibles conséquences [Immunopsychiatry and SARS-CoV-2 pandemic: Links and possible consequences]. *L'Encephale*, *47*(2), 151–156. https://doi.org/10.1016/j.encep.2020.07.002

Dursun, O. B., Turan, B., Pakyürek, M., & Tekin, A. (2021). Integrating telepsychiatric services into the conventional systems for psychiatric support to health care workers and their children during COVID-19 pandemics: Results from A national experience. *Telemedicine Journal and e-Health: The Official Journal of the American Telemedicine Association*, *27*(3), 269–275. https://doi.org/10.1089/tmj.2020.0237

Hjorth, S., Bromley, R., Ystrom, E., Lupattelli, A., Spigset, O., & Nordeng, H. (2019). Use and validity of child neurodevelopment outcome measures in studies on prenatal exposure to psychotropic and analgesic medications – A systematic review. *PLoS One*, *14*(7), e0219778. https://doi.org/10.1371/journal.pone.0219778

Johnson, A. L., Torgerson, T., Skinner, M., Hamilton, T., Tritz, D., & Vassar, M. (2020). An assessment of transparency and reproducibility-related research practices in otolaryngology. *The Laryngoscope*, *130*(8), 1894–1901. https://doi.org/10.1002/lary.28322

Justesen, T., Freyberg, J., & Schultz, A. (2021). Database selection and data gathering methods in systematic reviews of qualitative research regarding diabetes mellitus – An explorative study. *BMC Medical Research Methodology*, *21*(1), 94. https://doi.org/10.1186/s12874-021-01281-2

Kastner, M., Tricco, A. C., Soobiah, C., Lillie, E., Perrier, L., Horsley, T., Welch, V., Cogo, E., Antony, J., & Straus, S. E. (2012). What is the most appropriate knowledge synthesis method to conduct a review? Protocol for a scoping review. *BMC Medical Research Methodology*, *12*(1), 114. https://doi.org/10.1186/1471-2288-12-114

Kawabe, K., Hosokawa, R., Nakachi, K., Yoshino, A., Horiuchi, F., & Ueno, S. I. (2020). Making a brochure about coronavirus disease (COVID-19) for children with autism spectrum disorder and their family members. *Psychiatry and Clinical Neurosciences*, *74*(9), 498–499. https://doi.org/10.1111/pcn.13090

Levac, D., Colquhoun, H., & O'Brien, K. K. (2010). Scoping studies: Advancing the methodology. *Implementation Science*, *5*(1), 69. https://doi.org/10.1186/1748-5908-5-69

Manning, J., Billian, J., Matson, J., Allen, C., & Soares, N. (2021). Perceptions of families of individuals with autism spectrum disorder during the COVID-19 crisis. *Journal of Autism and Developmental Disorders*, *51*(8), 2920–2928. https://doi.org/10.1007/s10803-020-04760-5

Miyakawa, T. (2020). No raw data, no science: Another possible source of the reproducibility crisis. *Molecular Brain*, *13*(1), 24. https://doi.org/10.1186/s13041-020-0552-2

Moher, D., Liberati, A., Tetzlaff, J., & Altman, D. G., & Prisma Group. (2009). Preferred reporting items for systematic reviews and meta-analyses: The PRISMA statement. *PLoS Medicine*, *6*(7), e1000097. https://doi.org/10.1371/journal.pmed.1000097

Morris, G., Bortolasci, C. C., Puri, B. K., Olive, L., Marx, W., O'Neil, A., Athan, E., Carvalho, A., Maes, M., Walder, K., & Berk, M. (2021). Preventing the development of severe COVID-19 by modifying immunothrombosis. *Life Sciences*, *264*, 118617. https://doi.org/10.1016/j.lfs.2020.118617

Munn, Z., Peters, M. D., Stern, C., Tufanaru, C., McArthur, A., & Aromataris, E. (2018). Systematic review or scoping review? Guidance for authors when choosing between a systematic or scoping review approach. *BMC Medical Research Methodology*, *18*(1), 143. https://doi.org/10.1186/s12874-018-0611-x

Narzisi, A. (2020). Handle the autism spectrum condition during coronavirus (COVID-19) stay at home period: Ten tips for helping parents and caregivers of young children. *Brain Sciences*, *10*(4), 207. https://doi.org/10.3390/brainsci10040207

Okonya, O., Rorah, D., Tritz, D., Umberham, B., Wiley, M., & Vassar, M. (2020). Analysis of practices to promote reproducibility and transparency in anaesthesiology research. *British Journal of Anaesthesia*, *125*(5), 835–842. https://doi.org/10.1016/j.bja.2020.03.035

Pascariello, G., Cimino, G., Calvi, E., Bernardi, N., Grigolato, M., Garyfallidis, P., Fabbricatore, D., Pezzola, E., Lombardi, C. M., Metra, M., & Vizzardi, E. (2020). Cardiogenic shock due to COVID-19-related myocarditis in a 19-year-old autistic patient. *Journal of Medical Cases*, *11*(7), 207–210. https://doi.org/10.14740/jmc3517

Sheehan, R., Dalton-Locke, C., Ali, A., Vera San Juan, N., Totsika, V., & Hassiotis, A. (2021). Effects of the COVID-19 pandemic on mental healthcare and services: Results of a UK survey of front-line staff working with people with intellectual disability and/or autism. *BJPsych Bulletin*, 1–7. https://doi.org/10.1192/bjb.2021.52

Tamouza, R., Krishnamoorthy, R., & Leboyer, M. (2021). Understanding the genetic contribution of the human leukocyte antigen system to common major psychiatric disorders in a world pandemic context. *Brain, Behavior, and Immunity*, *91*, 731–739. https://doi.org/10.1016/j.bbi.2020.09.033

Tarbox, C. M., Silverman, E. A., Chastain, A. N., Little, A., Bermudez, T. L., & Tarbox, J. (2020). Taking ACTion: 18 simple strategies for supporting children with autism during the COVID-19 pandemic. *Behavior Analysis in Practice*, *14*(4), 1–29. https://doi.org/10.1007/s40617-020-00448-5

Wagner, L., Weitlauf, A. S., Hine, J., Corona, L. L., Berman, A. F., Nicholson, A., Allen, W., Black, M., & Warren, Z. (2022). Transitioning to telemedicine during COVID-19: Impact on perceptions and use of telemedicine procedures for the diagnosis of autism in toddlers. *Journal of Autism and Developmental Disorders*, *52*(5), 2247–2257. https://doi.org/10.1007/s10803-021-05112-7

Wang, C. (2020). The impact of COVID-19 on autism research: Reflections from China. *Autism: The International Journal of Research and Practice*, *13*(7), 1028. https://doi.org/10.1002/aur.2344

3

RESULTS

3.1 INTRODUCTION

This chapter furnishes the reader with the results of the *Preferred Reporting Items for Systematic Reviews and Meta-Analyses* (PRISMA) analysis process. It begins with a synopsis of the literature about the experiences of the COVID-19 pandemic from the perspective of parents raising autistic children. It then outlines findings from the collected literature about the impact of the COVID-19 pandemic on autistic children and autistic adults. The limitations in the current literature are then reported followed by an overview of three topics that only have a paucity of literature, which are vaccine hesitancy among autistics and parents raising autistic children, the experiences of autistics living with COVID-19 disease and parenting an autistic child during the COVID-19 pandemic. The overall purpose of this chapter is to provide a context for the findings that were collected in the online surveys that will be presented in the next chapter.

Keywords: Anxiety; COVID-19 disease; depression; homogeneous samples; interviews; lockdowns; methodological limitations; sample size; survey

3.2 WHAT ARE THE EXPERIENCES OF THE COVID-19 PANDEMIC FROM THE PERSPECTIVE OF PARENTS RAISING AUTISTIC CHILDREN?

After applying the PRISMA analysis process to the 188 citations collected from the PubMed search conducted on 4 July 2021 it was revealed that five studies contained insights from parents about raising autistic children during the COVID-19 pandemic. Two of these studies were conducted in the Kingdom of Saudi Arabia (Alhuzimi, 2021; Althiabi, 2021), while the others were conducted in the United States (Manning et al., 2021), Israel (Tokatly Latzer et al., 2021), and China (Wang et al., 2021). Wang et al. (2021) published the study with the largest number of participants (i.e. $n = 6726$) while Tokatly Latzer et al. (2021) published the study with the smallest number of participants (i.e. $n = 31$). One study had a control group (Wang et al., 2021) while the other four only contained samples of parents raising autistic children (Alhuzimi, 2021; Althiabi, 2021; Manning et al., 2021; Tokatly Latzer et al., 2021). Except for Tokatly Latzer et al.'s (2021) study, which used semi-structured telephone interviews, all other studies collected data from the participants via surveys (see Table 3.1). What follows now is a description of each study's aims, methods of data collection and results.

Table 3.1. Characteristics of Studies about Parents Raising Autistic Children.

Study	Location of Participants	No. of Participants	Data Collection Method
Alhuzimi (2021)	Saudi Arabia	140 (39 fathers, 111 mothers)	Survey
Althiabi (2021)	Saudi Arabia	211 (84 fathers, 127 mothers)	Survey
Manning et al. (2021)	USA	471	Survey
Tokatly Latzer et al. (2021)	Israel	31 (6 fathers, 25 mothers)	Semi-structured telephone interviews
Wang et al. (2021)	China	ASD family = 1,764 (246 fathers, 1,518 mothers) Control group = 4962 (771 fathers, 4,191 mothers)	Survey

Key: ASD = Autism Spectrum Disorder, USA = United States of America.

Two studies about the experiences of parents raising autistic children during the COVID-19 pandemic in the Kingdom of Saudi Arabia were identified (Alhuzimi, 2021; Althiabi, 2021). Using several surveys, Alhuzimi (2021) collected data from 140 parents (39 fathers, 111 mothers). They discovered that the age and gender of the autistic child and the level of their support needs had a significant impact on parental stress and emotional well-being. Specifically, parents raising young children with more support needs reported greater levels of stress than parents raising older children with fewer support needs. Second, the COVID-19 pandemic has decreased the overall emotional well-being of parents raising autistic children in the Kingdom of Saudi Arabia. Based on these results, Alhuzimi recommended that the Saudi Ministry of Health create and disseminate support programmes to help parents raising their autistic children during the COVID-19 pandemic.

Althiabi (2021) examined the attitude, anxiety and perceived mental health of parents raising autistic children in the Kingdom of Saudi Arabia during the COVID-19 pandemic. For their study 211 parents completed an online survey. They reported that the parents' level of anxiety was significantly greater than before the COVID-19 pandemic. Additionally, some of the parents' free-text responses to the questionnaire indicated that they sought advice from their children's teachers, other family members and therapists to help them raise their autistic children during the COVID-19 pandemic.

Manning et al. (2021) examined the stress that parents of autistic children experienced during the early stages of the COVID-19 pandemic. However, unlike Althiabi and Alhuzimi's studies, they conducted their study in Michigan instead of the Kingdom of Saudi Arabia. All parents raising autistic children who participated in their study were recruited from the Autism Alliance of Michigan (AAoM). Three days after a stay-at-home order was imposed in Michigan, Manning and colleagues distributed their survey to parents who belonged to the AAoM (n = 1000). Their survey was open from 26 March 2020 to 4 May 2020. In total, 471 respondents who resided across 58 counties in Michigan completed their survey. Like Alhuzimi's study, Manning and colleagues reported that parents raising younger autistic children with more support needs experienced more stress than parents who were raising older autistic children with fewer support needs. Additionally, isolation, illness and financial difficulties were the greatest areas of stress disclosed by the parents.

Like Manning et al., Tokatly Latzer et al. (2021) also asked parents how they and their autistic children were coping during a COVID-19 lockdown. During April 2020, 31 parents who were collectively raising 25 autistic children participated in telephone interviews. These interviews were conducted one month after a complete lockdown was imposed in Israel. The interview schedule contained 10 questions. Table 3.2 is a selection of the questions they were asked (see Table 3.2).

Tokatly Latzer and colleagues reported that a change in routines, lack of special education services, limited physical space associated with staying at home in confinement, and food- and sleep-related issues were the main factors that caused autistic children the most stress during the COVID-19 pandemic lockdown in Israel. Additionally, a parent's flexibility to accommodate to their

Table 3.2. Examples of Questions Asked during the Telephone Interviews.

Questions
What were your initial thoughts and feelings when the government announced the beginning of the lockdown and its details?
Possible follow-ups: What made you think/feel this way?
Did you experience any difficulties/benefits of the lockdown period so far?
Is he or she showing any understanding about what COVID-19 is and its implications?

Source: Tokatly Latzer et al. (2021, p. 1050).

child's needs, a creative and resourceful problem-solving orientation, and a general positive outlook were the most influential factors that determined if autistic children either adapted or not to the lockdown situation.

Unlike the previous studies, Wang et al. (2021) compared the resilience, coping strategies, anxiety and depressive symptoms of parents raising either autistic or non-autistic children during the COVID-19 pandemic from three provinces in China (i.e. Heilongjiang, Henan and Fujian). Based on the responses collected from their survey, Wang and colleagues reported that during the ongoing COVID-19 pandemic parents raising autistic children had lower levels of resilience and positive coping skills compared to the parents who were raising non-autistic children. Additionally, more parents raising autistic children exhibited anxiety (12.2%) and depression (31%) compared to parents raising non-autistic children (anxiety = 6.6%; depression = 21.7%).

3.3 WHAT IMPACTS HAS THE COVID-19 PANDEMIC HAD ON AUTISTICS?

The PRISMA analysis process revealed 16 studies about autistics and their experiences of the COVID-19 pandemic. Of these, nine documented parents describing their autistic children's experiences of the COVID-19 pandemic (see Table 3.3), five contained accounts of autistic adults recalling their experiences of this pandemic (see Table 3.6), and two contained a sample of both autistic adults and autistic children and their experiences of this pandemic (see Table 3.15).

3.3.1 Autistic Children

Of the nine studies that contained accounts of parents describing their autistic children's experiences of the COVID-19 pandemic, two were conducted in the United States (Corbett et al., 2021; Garcia et al., 2021), while one study was conducted in France (Berard et al., 2021), Italy (Colizzi et al., 2020), China (Huang et al., 2021), Japan (Kawabe et al., 2020), Spain (Mumbardó-Adam et al., 2021), Chile (Nuñez et al., 2021) and Turkey (Türkoğlu et al., 2020). The study with the largest sample of participants was published by Huang et al. (2021) ($n = 406$) while the study with the smallest sample of participants was published by Garcia et al. (2021) ($n = 9$). Two studies had a control group (Corbett et al., 2021; Kawabe et al., 2020). Finally, all studies collected data via surveys (see Table 3.3). What follows now is a description of each study's aims, methods of data collection and results.

Table 3.3. Studies That Contain Parental Accounts of Their Autistic Children and the COVID-19 Pandemic.

Study	Location of Participants	No. of Participants	Data Collection Method
Berard et al. (2021)	France	238 (34 male, 204 female)	Survey
Colizzi et al. (2020)	Italy	527	Survey
Corbett et al. (2021)	USA	TD children = 61 (35 male, 26 female) ASD children = 61 (46 male, 15 female)	Survey
Garcia et al. (2021)	USA*	9 (8 male, 1 female)	Survey
Huang et al. (2021)	China	406 parents	Survey
Kawabe et al. (2020)	Japan	ASD = 84 (63 male, 21 female) Control = 361 (217 male, 90 female)	Survey
Mumbardó-Adam et al. (2021)	Spain	47 (36 male, 11 female)	Survey
Nuñez et al. (2021)	Chile	118 (94 male, 24 female)	Survey
Türkoğlu et al. (2020)	Turkey	46 (38 male, 8 female)	Survey

Key: * Location of first author since location of participants was not stated in the study, ASD = Autism Spectrum Disorder, TD = Typically Developing, USA = United States of America.

Berard et al. (2021) examined the impact that lockdown measures had on autistic children's behaviours, communication, sleep and nutritional status. They also examined the risk and protective factors that influenced an autistic child's change in behaviours. To fulfil these objectives, they sent an invitation letter to all parents raising autistic children in the Elena network. If they accepted this invitation, they were then sent an online questionnaire to complete. Based on the statistical data collected, Berard and colleagues reported that an autistic child's age, level of support needs, single parenthood status and daily living skills had the greatest impact on their behaviours during the COVID-19 pandemic.

From the perspective of their parents, Colizzi et al. (2020) examined the impacts that the COVID-19 pandemic had on autistic children and if there were any pre-pandemic sociodemographic or clinical characteristics that contributed to negative outcomes. Parents or guardians of autistic children completed an online survey which contained 40 questions which measured clinical and sociodemographic characteristics of their autistic children, the impacts of the COVID-19 pandemic on the well-being of their autistic children and their autistic child's ability to deal with an emergency. In total, 527 parents completed the online survey. Overall, 93.9% of parents reported that their autistic child demonstrated increased difficulties during the COVID-19 pandemic. Specifically, they reported that their autistic children exhibited increased difficulties with managing their free time (78.1%) and presented more behaviour problems (41.5%). However, the COVID-19 pandemic had minimal impact on their autistic child's meal preparation or autonomy (see Table 3.4).

Table 3.4. Psychosocial and Behavioural Impact of the Emergency Outbreak.

Question	*N*	%
COVID-19 positivity among nuclear family members		
No	519	98.7
Yes	7	1.3
Missing	1	
COVID-19 positivity among extended family members		
No	500	95.6
Yes	23	4.4
Missing	4	

Table 3.4. *(Continued)*

Question	***N***	**%**
Bereavement due to COVID-19		
No	514	97.7
Yes	12	2.3
Missing	1	
Mother's current working situation		
Regularly commuting to work	92	17.6
Smart working	98	18.7
Not working because of COVID-19	137	26.1
Not working since before COVID-19	197	37.6
Missing	3	
Father's current working situation		
Regularly commuting to work	212	42
Smart working	104	20.6
Not working because of COVID-19	139	27.5
Not working since before COVID-19	50	9.9
Missing	22	
Judgement on this period of change and restrictions		
Very challenging	284	54
Challenging	210	39.9
Not challenging	32	6.1
Missing	1	
Judgement on this period of change and restrictions as compared to before COVID-19		
More challenging	405	77
Equally challenging	86	16.3
Less challenging	35	6.7
Missing	1	
Support by Local Healthcare Services since COVID-19		
Daily contacts	7	1.4
Weekly contacts	98	19.4
Twice weekly contacts	35	6.9
No contact	366	72.3
Missing	21	
Usefulness of support by Local Healthcare Services during COVID-19		
Very useful	10	2.2
Useful	28	6.1

Table 3.4. (*Continued*)

Question	***N***	**%**
Sufficiently useful	65	14.1
Not very useful	93	20.1
Not useful	266	57.6
Missing	65	
Direct school support since COVID-19		
Daily contacts	110	22.5
Weekly contacts	157	32.3
Twice weekly contacts	75	15.4
No contact	146	29.9
Missing	39	
Indirect school support since COVID-19		
Daily contacts	138	28.7
Weekly contacts	159	33.1
Twice weekly contacts	106	22.1
No contact	77	16
Missing	47	
Usefulness of school support during COVID-19		
Very useful	60	12.9
Useful	113	24.4
Sufficiently useful	116	25
Not very useful	93	20
Not useful	82	17.7
Missing	63	
Private therapist support since COVID-19		
Daily contacts	43	12.6
Weekly contacts	148	43.4
Twice weekly contacts	59	17.3
No contact	91	26.7
Missing	1	
Usefulness of private therapist during COVID-19		
Very useful	65	19.6
Useful	80	24.1
Sufficiently useful	64	19.3
Not very useful	50	15.1
Not useful	73	22

Table 3.4. *(Continued)*

Question	*N*	%
Missing		
Difficulties in managing the child's meals since COVID-19		
No	404	77
Yes	121	23
Missing	2	
Greater difficulties in managing the child's meals as compared to before COVID-19		
No	378	71.9
Yes	148	28.1
Missing	1	
Difficulties in managing the child's autonomies since COVID-19		
No	361	69
Yes	162	31
Missing	4	
Greater difficulties in managing the child's autonomies as compared to before COVID-19		
No	372	71
Yes	152	29
Missing	3	
Difficulties in managing the child's free time since COVID-19		
No	115	21.9
Yes	411	78.1
Missing	1	
Greater difficulties in managing the child's free time as compared to before COVID-19		
No	97	18.4
Yes	429	81.6
Missing	1	
Difficulties in managing the child's structured activities since COVID-19		
No	126	24.3
Yes	393	75.7
Missing	8	
Greater difficulties in managing the child's structured activities as compared to before COVID-19		
No	123	23.8
Yes	394	76.2
Missing	10	

Table 3.4. (*Continued*)

Question	***N***	**%**
Intensity of the child's behaviour problems as compared to before COVID-19		
More intense	183	35.5
Equally intense	264	51.3
Less intense	68	13.2
Missing	12	
Frequency of the child's behaviour problems as compared to before COVID-19		
More frequent	216	41.5
Equally frequent	229	44
Less frequent	76	14.6
Missing	6	
Contacts with the child's neuropsychiatrist due to behavioural problems since COVID-19		
No	424	80.9
Yes	100	19.1
Missing	3	
Access to A&E for child's behavioural problems since COVID-19		
No	514	98.5
Yes	8	1.5
Missing	5	

Source: Colizzi et al. (2020, pp. 6–9).

Of the 527 respondents who completed the online survey for Colizzi and colleagues' study, 406 (77%) reported at least one support option that could be of help to them when raising their autistic child during the ongoing COVID-19 pandemic. Additionally, 10 respondents reported more than one support option (i.e. four respondents reported two needs and six respondents reported three needs). The most reported need was in-home healthcare support (n = 126, 29.9%), followed by centre-based healthcare support (n = 44, 10.4%), loosening quarantine restrictions (n = 41, 9.7%), ending lockdown (n = 30, 7.1%) and in-hospital healthcare support (n = 30, 7.1%) (see Table 3.5).

Table 3.5. Responses to the Open-Response Question about What Could Be of Help to Deal with the Ongoing Emergency.

	N	%
In-home healthcare support	126	29.9
Centre-based healthcare support	44	10.4
Loosening quarantine restrictions	41	9.7
Ending lockdown	30	7.1
In-hospital healthcare support	30	7.1
Increase school support	29	6.9
Help setting a daily schedule	21	5
'Nothing'	20	4.7
'Don't know'	14	3.3
Parent support	13	3.1
Peer relationship	12	2.8
Structured physical activity	9	2.1
Community support	9	2.1
Financial family support	8	1.9
Work support	6	1.4
Spiritual and religious reflections	4	0.9
Information technology support	3	0.7
Pharmacological support	3	0.7

Source: Colizzi et al. (2020, pp. 10–11).

Huang et al. (2021) examined the impact that the ongoing COVID-19 pandemic has had on autistic children and their families. They designed and distributed to six hospitals in south, east, central and western China an online survey that respondents could complete from 12 May 2020 to 31 May 2020. They reported that during the COVID-19 lockdown most parents (50.3%) thought that their autistic children experienced sleeping problems and 47.3% thought that their autistic children's outside activities were reduced. Almost 40% of parents thought that their autistic child's cognitive abilities, language abilities and expression, and understanding improved. In contrast, some parents (36.2%) believed that their autistic children's emotional and social states worsened during lockdown.

Mumbardó-Adam et al. (2021) examined autistic children/adolescents and their parents' management of COVID-19 quarantine procedures. In total, 47 families with autistic children who lived in a northern region of Spain participated in the study. Data were collected via an online survey that was filled out during April 2020. Arguably, one of the most striking findings was that most respondents claimed that during quarantine their autistic children were happier than before quarantine.

> *The majority [of autistic children] seemed to be comfortable with the situation and did not often ask to go back to school or to previous routines. Families also benefited from this extra time with their sons and daughters to teach new skills related to their autonomy, to house care routines, and perhaps more importantly, to social skills and communicative interaction.*
>
> *(Mumbardó-Adam et al., 2021, p. 6)*

Nuñez et al. (2021) published a brief study in which they reported the impact of the start of the COVID-19 pandemic on the intensity and frequency of behavioural problems of autistic children living in Chile. In total, 118 parents raising autistic children completed their online survey, which could be completed from 1 August 2020 to 30 October 2020. Based on the responses collected, 44.9% of parents claimed that at the start of the COVID-19 pandemic their autistic children displayed more intense and frequent behavioural problems.

Türkoğlu et al. (2020) examined the impact of a COVID-19 pandemic lockdown in Turkey on the sleep and behaviour problems of 46 autistic children (38 boys, eight girls) not taking medication who were aged 4–17 years. They collected data using a survey that was distributed to eligible parents raising autistic children from 7 May 2020 to 14 May 2020. The responses showed that autistic children exhibited sleep problems during the COVID-19 pandemic lockdown.

In the studies explained previously, parents provided answers about their autistic children. However, for Garcia et al.'s (2021) study autistic adolescents instead provided their insights about the impacts that the COVID-19 pandemic had on their physical activity, time spent watching a screen, and total sleep time. They were recruited during March 2020, a few weeks prior to the quarantine period for the COVID-19 pandemic. The week quarantine began, the autistic adolescents received a link to the electronic survey. Their survey contained three components, which were:

(1) *Physical activity*: Respondents were asked 'How many days per week do you participate in at least 60 min of physical activity?' Respondents were asked to recall their physical activity for the previous zero to seven days.

(2) *Screen time*: To measure the amount of time that the respondent watched a screen, each respondent was asked 'How many hours of screen time (television, computer, iphone, ipad, etc.) did you spend on a typical weekday?' Respondents were also asked to comment on the amount of time that they watched a screen during the weekend. However, they were asked not to count the number of hours that they were using electronic devices for schoolwork, such as computers.

(3) *Sleep duration*: For a typical weekday and weekend respondents were asked to report the times they went to bed and woke up. For both weekdays and weekends the amount of sleep time was calculated by counting the hours between the reported time they went to bed and woke up.

For their study autistic adolescents completed the same survey at two different times. For the first survey, distributed during early March 2020, respondents were asked to not consider the current circumstances surrounding the pandemic but their physical activity, screen time and total sleep duration for the past week. Towards the end of April, six weeks after the first survey was administered, the same survey was re-administered. Whilst completing the re-administered survey respondents were asked to consider the impact that the quarantine period had on their activities. Furthermore, unlike the first survey, the re-administered survey contained two additional questions, which were:

(1) As a result of the pandemic and quarantine, do you feel your physical activity increased/decreased/did not change?

(2) As a result of the pandemic and quarantine, do you feel your screen time habits increased/decreased/did not change?

For Garcia et al.'s study, nine autistic adolescents (eight males, one female) completed both surveys. Regarding physical activity, seven (78%) reported that their physical activity had decreased, one (11%) claimed that the amount for physical activity they did had not changed and one (11%) stated that their physical activity had increased. Regarding screen time, one (11%) disclosed that the amount of time that they had spent watching a screen had decreased, one (11%) revealed no change and seven (78%) recalled that they spent more time watching a screen during the COVID-19 pandemic. Finally, four of the nine respondents (44%) reported that they were going to bed later than usual. However, three (75%) of these four respondents claimed that they were waking up later in the day as well. Based on these findings, Garcia et al. (2021, p. 4) concluded that:

> *Although preliminary, this study is the first to provide evidence that adolescents with ASD may experience significant decreases in physical activity, and increases in levels of screen time during the COVID-19 outbreak. As the duration of the pandemic is unknown, it is critical to understand the effects of COVID-19 on health behaviors in youth with ASD, so that effective strategies can be developed to attenuate the negative impact and protect against possible long-term health risks from the current outbreak, and future events of similar magnitude.*

An examination of the contents of the studies identified from the PRISMA analysis revealed two studies that contained a control group (Corbett et al., 2021; Kawabe et al., 2020). For Corbett et al.'s (2021) study, 61 autistic children and their parents and 61 non-autistic children and their parents provided their insights about their stress, anxiety and coping related to the COVID-19 pandemic. Data were collected from participants via an online survey at three points in time. For Time 0, respondents provided information before the COVID-19 lockdown. For Time 1, respondents were asked to focus on their experience of the COVID-19 pandemic from 27 April 2020 to 29 May 2020. These dates encapsulated the initial peak of the stay-at-home orders across the United States and Tennessee. For Time 2, respondents were asked to provide answers based on their experiences from 2 August 2020 to 10 September 2020. This date range covered the partial, phased-based re-opening of the community, including a new beginning of the school year. Corbett and colleagues reported that autistic children reported more anxiety and stress during the COVID-19 pandemic lockdown than non-autistic children. Parents raising autistic children reported greater rates of self-reported anxiety and stress than parents raising non-autistic children during the COVID-19 pandemic.

Kawabe et al. (2020) compared the internet and digital media usage before and during the COVID-19 pandemic between 84 autistic children and 361 non-autistic children who were both age- and gender-matched. For their study, mothers raising autistic or non-autistic children completed the online survey that was available from 30 April 2020 to 8 May 2020. They reported that excessive internet usage occurred among autistics and non-autistics during the COVID-19 pandemic. Before this pandemic, autistic children spent an average of three hours watching a screen while non-autistic children spent two hours. In contrast, during this pandemic autistic children spent an average of five hours watching a screen while non-autistic children spent four hours.

3.3.2 Autistic Adults

Of the five studies about autistic adults describing their experiences of the COVID-19 pandemic, three were conducted in the United States (Adams et al., 2021; Bal et al., 2021; Pfeiffer et al., 2022), one was conducted in Israel (Goldfarb et al., 2022), and one was conducted across three countries (Oomen et al., 2021). Oomen et al.'s (2021) study contained the largest number of participants (*n* = 1044), possibly because they recruited participants from three countries (i.e. Belgium, the Netherlands and the United Kingdom). In contrast, Pfeiffer et al.'s (2022) study contained the smallest number of participants (*n* = 6). One study had a control group (Oomen et al., 2021) and four studies collected data at multiple points in time (Adams et al., 2021; Bal et al., 2021; Goldfarb et al., 2022; Pfeiffer et al., 2022). Finally, the data in all studies were collected via surveys. However, Goldfarb et al. (2022) also collected data from interviews (see Table 3.6). Each study's aims, methods of data collection and results are now outlined.

Table 3.6. Studies that Contain Accounts from Autistic Adults about the COVID-19 Pandemic.

Study	Location of Participants	No. of Participants	Data Collection Method
Adams et al. (2021)	USA	275 (140 male, 35 female)	Survey
Bal et al. (2021)	USA*	396	Survey
Goldfarb et al. (2022)	Israel	Survey at T1 = 34 (30 male, 4 female) Survey at T2 = 23 (19 male, 4 female)	Mixed Methods
Oomen et al. (2021)	Belgium, the Netherlands and the United Kingdom	ASD group = 613 (204 male, 409 female) Control group = 431 (122 male, 309 female)	Survey
Pfeiffer et al. (2022)	USA*	6 (4 male, 2 female)	Survey

Key: * Location of first author since location of participants was not stated in the study, ASD = autism spectrum disorder, T1 = Time 1, T2 = Time 2, USA = United States of America.

Adams et al. (2021) measured the levels of stress that 275 autistic adults who lived in the United States experienced before and 10 weeks into the COVID-19 pandemic. Ten weeks before the lockdown (i.e. Time 1: 11 March 2020 to 20 March 2020) 316 autistic adults completed their online survey. Ten weeks into the COVID-19 pandemic (i.e. Time 2: 18 May 2020 to 27 May 2020), 275 of the 316 autistic adults (87.3%) who completed the survey for Time 1 also completed the survey for Time 2. For Time 1 and 2, all participants completed the Lovibond and Lovibond's *Depression Anxiety Stress Scale*. This scale contained 42 questions that measured depressed mood, lack of interests in daily abilities, hope in life, anxious feelings, somatic experiences related to anxiety, general stress, and stress-induced actions and emotions. During Time 2, participants answered two additional questions about the influence that the COVID-19 pandemic had on their development of stress. These questions were:

(1) How well are you coping with the changes happening in your life due to COVID-19? The participant's responses were coded as either 'coping well' (i.e. I am coping very well, I am coping well) or 'difficulty coping' (i.e. I am having some difficulty coping, I am having lots of difficulty coping).

(2) To what extent has your emotional or mental health been negatively impacted by COVID-19? The participant's responses were coded as either 'low negative impact' (i.e. minimal impact or not at all) or 'high negative impact' (i.e. severely impacted or moderately impacted).

Of the 275 participants who provided answers for Time 2, 270 (98.2%) answered the two COVID-19 questions. Additionally, 178 (65%) claimed that the COVID-19 pandemic had contributed to their distress, 138 (50%) reported that they had difficulty adapting to the COVID-19 pandemic, and 157 (57%) claimed that the COVID-19 pandemic has had a negative impact on their emotional and mental health. Due to these findings, Adams et al. (2021, p. 1) concluded that:

> *...adults with higher levels of anxiety prior to the pandemic were more likely to report distress, and women were more likely to report a negative impact of the pandemic on their emotional and mental health.*

Bal et al. (2021) examined if an autistic's characteristics (e.g. demographics, location, or previous mental health diagnosis) contributed to them experiencing a negative impact during the COVID-19 pandemic. They also sought to discover the factors that either influenced or prevented the development of psychological distress among autistics during the early months of the COVID-19 pandemic. They hypothesised that higher levels of distress during the COVID-19 pandemic were more likely if the autistic participant had a personal experience of COVID-19, such as knowing someone with COVID-19. In total, 3133 autistic adults were invited to complete a brief online survey about the impact that the COVID-19 pandemic has had on their lives. Each participant was required to complete two separate surveys. The first survey was available from 30 March 2020 to 10 April 2020 while the second survey was available from 27 May 2020 to 6 June 2020.

A comparison of the data collected from the first and second survey revealed that those who reported the greatest negative impacts of the COVID-19 pandemic were female, had a prior diagnosis of a co-morbid mental health condition, were younger and had a personal experience of COVID-19 (i.e. knowing someone who had COVID-19 symptoms or who had tested positive for COVID-19) (Bal et al., 2021).

Goldfarb et al. (2022) examined the COVID-19 pandemic's impacts on the employment status and work arrangements (e.g. layoffs, remote work from home or furloughs) of autistic adults. Satisfaction with the job, mental health and employment-related psychological needs were also examined. To fulfil this objective Goldfarb and colleagues proposed two hypotheses, which were as follows:

(1) Working conditions will worsen for autistic employees, i.e. higher unemployment rates and negative changes in work conditions will be found.

(2) Job satisfaction, employment-related psychological need satisfaction and mental health will deteriorate in relation to pre-COVID-19 reports.

Data were collected from the participants on three occasions:

- *Time 1:* From September 2019 to January 2020 data were collected before the COVID-19 pandemic started in Israel.
- *Time 2:* From April 2020 to May 2020 all 34 participants who completed the survey for Time 1 were invited to provide data for Time 2. Out of the 34 participants invited, 23 (67%) completed the survey for Time 2.
- *Time 3:* During October 2020, the third phase of data collection occurred. All 16 participants who reported being employed during Time 2 were invited to participate in a brief interview or answer an open-ended questionnaire. Ten participants (eight males, two females) responded.

Based on the responses collected, Goldfarb and colleagues concluded that there was a significant reduction in the mental health of the participants who lost their jobs during the COVID-19 pandemic. Additionally, a marginally significant deterioration in mental health was measured among participants who engaged in work-from-home arrangements.

Pfeiffer et al. (2022) examined the impact of the COVID-19 pandemic lockdowns on the mobility of six autistic adults (four males, two females) between the ages of 21–27 years. All participants were provided with a Global Positioning System (GPS)-enabled mobile phone that continuously recorded their location during the data collection periods. Additionally, all participants completed an online survey about their location. The participants' location was collected two weeks before the initial COVID-19 lockdown started (i.e. from 3 January 2020 to 29 February 2020), during the start of the COVID-19 lockdown (i.e. from 20 March 2020 to 2 April 2020) and then later (i.e. from 20 April 2020 to 3 May 2020). However, one participant only had two tracking periods (i.e. from 3 January 2020 to 29 February 2020 and from 20 April 2020 to 3 May 2020). The GPS and survey data revealed that during the COVID-19 lockdown all participants had a decrease in the distance that they travelled, which is a consequence of the lockdown restrictions. Despite this relatively obvious finding, the researchers did not explore the emotional consequences of the lockdown on autistics.

Unlike the four previous studies, Oomen et al. (2021) collected data from participants who lived in three countries (i.e. Belgium, the Netherlands, and the United Kingdom) during one occasion. Oomen et al.'s study had three objectives. First, to measure the impact of the COVID-19 pandemic on the depression and anxiety of autistic adults. Second, to measure the impact of the COVID-19 pandemic on the everyday life and routines of autistic adults. Third, to evaluate the usefulness of pandemic-related information and whether the participants received appropriate guidance or had a desire to receive such guidance during the ongoing pandemic. To achieve these objectives, they distributed a survey to autistic and non-autistic respondents who lived in either Belgium, the Netherlands or the United Kingdom. In total, 1044 respondents completed their survey. Of these, 517 (49.5%) lived in Belgium, 244 (23.4%) lived in the Netherlands and 283 (27.1%) lived in the United Kingdom. Furthermore, 613 adults were in the autistic group while 431 adults were in the non-autistic group. Adapted versions of the *Patient Health Questionnaire-9* (PHQ-9) and the *Generalised Anxiety Disorder Scale* (GAD-7) were distributed to respondents to measure their anxiety and depression during the COVID-19 pandemic. The results showed that autistic adults were more anxious and depressed during this pandemic than non-autistics, as indicated by elevated scores on all subscales of the PHQ-9 and GAD-7 (Oomen et al., 2021) (see Table 3.7).

All participants completed a questionnaire about typical worries that they may have had over the past two weeks during the COVID-19 pandemic. The results indicated that worries about their pets, work (even when they felt that their job was safe), getting medication and food, and own safety/security were more elevated amongst autistic adults than that of non-autistic adults. However, autistic adults were less anxious than non-autistic adults about COVID-19 pandemic-specific worries (Oomen et al., 2021) (see Table 3.8).

Table 3.7. COVID-19 Pandemic-Related Change in Depression and Anxiety Symptoms.

	Autistic *M* (SD)	Non-autistic *M* (SD)
Depression symptoms		
Total *adapted* PHQ-9 score	3.57 (0.71)	3.30 (0.56)
Little interest or pleasure doing things	3.41 (1.06)	3.27 (0.86)
Feeling down, depressed or hopeless	3.70 (1.07)	3.42 (0.89)
Trouble falling or staying asleep or too much sleep	3.86 (1.02)	3.51 (0.94)
Feeling tired or having little energy	3.79 (1.03)	3.46 (0.96)
Poor appetite or overeating	3.71 (0.91)	3.46 (0.80)
Feeling bad about yourself – or that you are a failure or have let yourself or your family down	3.54 (1.05)	3.31 (0.81)
Trouble concentrating on things, such as reading the newspaper or watching television	3.59 (1.00)	3.26 (0.79)
Moving or speaking so slowly that other people could have noticed	3.26 (0.77)	3.01 (0.56)
Thought that you would be better off dead or of hurting yourself	3.22 (0.95)	2.97 (0.70)
Impact: How difficult have these problems made it for you to do your work, take care of things at home or get along with other people[a]	2.39 (0.89)	1.82 (0.73)
Anxiety symptoms		
Total *adapted* GAD-7 score	3.62 (0.82)	3.38 (0.60)
Feeling nervous, anxious or on edge	3.77 (1.06)	3.58 (0.87)
Not being able to stop or control worrying	3.63 (1.00)	3.40 (0.78)
Worrying too much about different things	3.67 (1.01)	3.41 (0.75)
Trouble relaxing	3.66 (1.03)	3.39 (0.87)
Being so restless that it's hard to sit still	3.31 (0.91)	3.06 (0.64)
Becoming easily annoyed or irritable	3.64 (1.05)	3.46 (0.87)
Feeling afraid as if something awful might happen	3.63 (0.97)	3.39 (0.75)
Impact: How difficult have these problems made it for you to do your work, take care of things at home or get along with other people?[a]	2.39 (0.88)	1.85 (0.69)

Key: Autistic group: $n = 613$, non-autistic group: $n = 431$; Questions were rated on a five-point scale going from 1 ('significantly less than usual') to 5 ('significantly more than usual'), except for the additional impact questions that were rated on a four-point rating scale going from 1 ('not difficult at all') to 4 ('extremely difficult').

[a]Only includes participants that indicated 'slightly/significantly more than usual' to any of the above items. *Adapted* PHQ-9: autistic group $n = 524$, non-autistic group $n = 340$; *adapted* GAD-7: autistic group $n = 504$, non-autistic group $n = 330$.

Source: Oomen et al. (2021, p. 7).

Table 3.8. Mean Scores per Group Regarding Eleven General and Three Pandemic-Related Topics of Worry.

	Autistic *M* (SD)	Non-autistic *M* (SD)	LMM Statistics
Over the past 2 weeks, have you been more or less worried about the following?			
Marriage or other romantic relationship(s)	3.22 (0.90)	3.11 (0.86)	$\beta = -0.12$, χ^2 (1) = 1.33, $p = 0.248$, $q = 0.313$
Your pet[a]	3.25 (0.84)	2.99 (0.76)	$\beta = -0.32$, χ^2 (1) = 13.62, $p < 0.001$, $q = 0.001$
Work (even if you feel your job is safe)[b]	3.91 (0.96)	3.60 (1.03)	$\beta = -0.31$, χ^2 (1) = 14.33, $p < 0.001$, $q = 0.001$
Losing your job[b]	3.52 (1.04)	3.24 (0.99)	$\beta = -0.28$, χ^2 (1) = 8.19, $p = 0.004$, $q = 0.008$
Finances	3.56 (0.94)	3.45 (0.91)	$\beta = -0.12$, χ^2 (1) = 3.25, $p = 0.071$, $q = 0.101$
Getting medication	3.54 (0.87)	3.25 (0.69)	$\beta = -0.35$, χ^2 (1) = 28.51, $p < 0.001$, $q < 0.001$
Getting food	3.92 (0.92)	3.48 (0.83)	$\beta = -0.46$, χ^2 (1) = 9.06, $p = 0.003$, $q = 0.006$
Your own safety/security	3.75 (0.97)	3.57 (0.81)	$\beta = -0.23$, χ^2 (1) = 4.93, $p = 0.026$, $q = 0.048$
Internet access	3.24 (0.76)	3.16 (0.64)	$\beta = -0.08$, χ^2 (1) = 0.46, $p = 0.500$, $q = 0.571$
Boredom	3.38 (1.06)	3.37 (0.94)	$\beta = -0.01$, χ^2 (1) = 0.01, $p = 0.922$, $q = 0.962$
Future plans	3.88 (1.06)	3.87 (0.94)	$\beta = 0.02$, χ^2 (1) = 0.08, $p = 0.774$, $q = 0.844$
Over the past 2 weeks, have you been worried about the following?			
Following the recommendations to prevent spread of COVID-19 correctly	3.03 (1.45)	2.83 (1.29)	$\beta = -0.14$, χ^2 (1) = 3.75, $p = 0.053$, $q = 0.079$
Catching COVID-19	3.09 (1.36)	3.01 (1.24)	$\beta = -0.10$, χ^2 (1) = 0.75, $p = 0.388$, $q = 0.465$
Friends or family catching COVID-19	3.82 (1.26)	3.82 (1.13)	$\beta = -0.00$, χ^2 (1) = 0.00, $p = 0.974$, $q = 0.974$

Key: Autistic group: $n = 613$, non-autistic group: $n = 431$; Questions were rated on a five-point scale going from 1 ('significantly less than usual') to 5 ('significantly more than usual'), except for the COVID-19 pandemic-specific worries that were rated on a five-point scale going from 1 ('not at all') to 5 ('very much so'). Participants were asked to indicate 'not more than usual' when not applicable.

[a]Analysis only includes participants who indicated to have a pet, autistic group $n = 349$, non-autistic group $n = 209$.

[b]Analysis only includes participants who indicated to be self-, part-time, or full-time employed, autistic group $n = 306$, non-autistic group $n = 300$.

Source: Oomen et al. (2021, p. 8).

The results collected by Oomen and colleagues showed that the COVID-19 pandemic has disrupted the social and daily routines of both autistic and non-autistic adults. They reported that autistic adults were less inclined to feel that the COVID-19 pandemic had changed their social life than non-autistic adults. Additionally, during the COVID-19 pandemic autistic adults felt more relief from social stress while non-autistic adults felt more socially isolated. Regarding daily routines during the COVID-19 pandemic, autistic adults felt that they did not need to make many adjustments to their daily routines compared to non-autistic adults. Nonetheless, non-autistic adults felt less stressed when they had to change their daily routines compared to autistic adults (Oomen et al., 2021) (see Table 3.9).

Table 3.9. Mean Scores per Group Regarding the Impact of the Pandemic on Topics Related to the DSM Criteria of Autism Spectrum Disorder.

	Autistic *M* (SD)	Non-autistic *M* (SD)
Social contact (domain I)		
To what extent did the COVID-19 pandemic change your social life?	3.16 (1.41)	3.91 (1.17)
Due to the effects of the COVID-19 regulations on my everyday life, I feel socially isolated	2.59 (1.48)	2.89 (1.28)
Due to the effects of the COVID-19 regulations on my everyday life, I feel relieved from social stress	3.43 (1.43)	2.67 (1.30)
Routines (domain II)		
To what extent do you feel you have/had to adjust your daily routines due to the COVID-19 pandemic?	3.49 (1.27)	3.90 (1.08)
Due to the effects of the COVID-19 regulations on my everyday life, I feel stressed about changes to my daily routines	3.31 (1.39)	2.58 (1.24)
Due to the effects of the COVID-19 regulations on my everyday life, I enjoy the freedom to deviate from society's expectations and to adjust my routines to my personal preference	3.46 (1.39)	3.16 (1.30)

Key: Autistic group: n = 613, non-autistic group: n = 431; Questions were rated on a five-point scale going from 1 ('Not at all') to 5 ('Very much so').

Source: Oomen et al. (2021, p. 8).

The COVID-19 pandemic has inhibited people's access to medical and psychological services. Autistic adults (n = 169, 27.6%) were more inclined to cancel their mental health and psychology appointments due to the COVID-19 pandemic than non-autistic adults (n = 46, 10.7%). Interestingly, most autistic adults (n = 49, 50%) and non-autistic adults (n = 40, 72.7%) reported that the help and guidance that they wanted from healthcare professionals was unrelated to the COVID-19 pandemic (Oomen et al., 2021) (see Table 3.10).

Table 3.10. Responses to Questions Related to Help and Guidance.

	Autistic *n* (%)	**Non-autistic *n* (%)**
Did you receive any help/guidance from a qualified medical specialist (e.g. psychiatrist, psychologist, counsellor)?		
No, and I wouldn't want to	142 (23.2)	277 (64.3)
No, but I would like to	98 (16.0)	55 (12.8)
Yes, but sessions are cancelled due to the COVID-19 pandemic	169 (27.6)	46 (10.7)
Yes, and sessions are continuing (face-to-face or online)	204 (33.3)	53 (12.3)
If indicated 'no, but I would like to': *Is your wish to receive help/guidance related or unrelated to the pandemic*		
Related	8 (8.2)	6 (10.9)
Unrelated	49 (50.0)	40 (72.7)
Both unrelated and related	41 (41.8)	9 (16.4)

Key: Autistic group: n = 613, non-autistic group: n = 431.

Source: Oomen et al. (2021, p. 9).

For Oomen et al.'s (2021) study all autistic adults were asked 'What measures could be taken to help you manage your mental health during the current COVID-19 pandemic?' In response to this question, they expressed a desire for ongoing affordable and accessible professional support from healthcare professionals (e.g. medical, psychological and household support). Despite many needing to access this professional support for the first time they were unsure as to how to obtain it. Additionally, many who received these supports before the COVID-19 pandemic lost either all or most of these supports after this pandemic started (Oomen et al., 2021) (see Table 3.11).

Table 3.11. Themes Identified From Responses of Autistic Adults to the Following Open Question: What Measures Could Be Taken to Help You Manage Your Mental Health during the Current COVID-19 Pandemic?

Theme	Subtheme	Example Quote
(Continued) professional support		'I need to talk to my psychologist from time to time, but this is impossible right now as it is "not essential"' p. 38 'Would be nice if a professional checked up, helped with implementing tips and tools and some measure of reassurance was possible'. p. 148 'Help with nuanced issues arising from the pandemic—changes to social codes, how to behave around others'. p. 171
	Affordable and accessible	'More easily accessible and affordable psychological/therapeutic help (via Skype, chat . . .)'. p. 318
	Availability of various communication mediums	'Something that would help me and many others would be if access to primary healthcare was available by some means other than making a phone call—e.g. SMS, online text chat, etc. Like a lot of autistic people, I have a lot of anxiety about making or receiving phone calls. If I need healthcare I have to agree to answer a phone call at an unspecified time. If I don't answer, no healthcare. This is very difficult to contemplate'. p. 407
	Help structuring days	'Help with creating a routine to fit the pandemic and change'. p. 333
Clearer information and rules		'It would help me a lot if the rules were much clearer. It would avoid a lot of stress' [Translated] p. 942 'Difficulty in applying rules, because they are often ambiguous or too vague (what is still allowed, what is not). You think it's clear, and then someone else in the media brings up with his or her own opinion about those rules, making it a mess. I think that for me the extra stress that occurs from COVID-19 concerns social stress because of the new but unclear rules, and not stress by the virus itself'. [Translated] p. 27

Table 3.11. (*Continued*)

Theme	Subtheme	Example Quote
	Autism-tailored information and advice	'ASD Societies contacting individuals who are registered with them to advise them of the situation'. p. 8 'The only tips and tricks that are easily available for people with ASD are catered towards children or people with ASD and learning disabilities'. p. 224 'I was not aware that there were tips and tools for people with ASD specifically. Being made aware of these things might help'. p. 415

Source: Oomen et al. (2021, p. 10).

Many autistic adults explained that before the onset of the COVID-19 pandemic they had daily or weekly routines that gave them stability and a sense of security. However, when this pandemic started, they stopped these routines, which consequently had a detrimental impact on their mental health. Autistic and non-autistic adults both explained the detrimental impacts that the COVID-19 pandemic has had on their social lives. Some autistic adults explained that a lack of social contact resulted in their social skills regressing. Similarly, some autistic adults explained that because of the requirement to wear face masks this reduced their ability to read another person's facial expressions (Oomen et al., 2021) (see Table 3.12).

Table 3.12. Themes Identified from Responses of Autistic Adults to the Following Open Question: What Changes, Due to the Effects of the COVID-19 Regulations on Your Everyday Life, Are the Most Difficult for You (If Any)?

Theme	Example Quote
Loss of routine	'Usually I try to have five (sometimes short) live contacts every day, as otherwise I get lonely, which isn't possible right now. I usually also have fixed events (library, movie, class, market.) that give structure to my life, which I've also lost'. [Translated] p. 1

Table 3.12. *(Continued)*

Theme	Example Quote
	'Every form of external structure to my days have disappeared. Since I don't do well having to structure my day by myself, I'm not doing well with that'. p. 610 'Knowing that I can't go out even if I would normally choose not to is hard. It's also hard not following normal routines and meeting with people I would normally. I had just started going to a group to help with my social interaction which has had to stop. It's hard knowing I was making positive steps towards improving my social interactions and I've had to pause it. I know it is a needed measure to stop the virus but it's still hard'. p. 205 'Almost everything that was in my diary has fallen away. The first days after the measures were announced, and subsequently when they were being made stricter, I had to keep scratching things, until there was almost nothing left. All that unstructured time to be planned in again makes me very agitated'. [Translated] p. 14
Loss of social contact	'The stress of not being able to see loved ones outside the house and feeling crippled by social isolation, with no idea when it'll end. I feel a neurotypical person in this situation will have a vast number of people to interact with in varying ways. I have 2 who I'm in touch with outside my home and only 1 is via Skype. As an autistic I have a limited social circle and now it's even smaller, I worry about autistics who live alone consistently too'. p. 257 'The smallest social things I have managed to do so far (even if that is only one hug a month) from which I receive support, are now completely gone'. [Translated] p. 25 'The lack of social and physical contact is debilitating. And the uncertainty about how long I have to keep this up takes me into a downward spiral'. [translated] p. 2 'I've kind of liked having my own "sanctuary" at my house and being able to control my involvement with others but I am human, despite autism, and I am starting to miss the option of socializing'. p. 977

Source: Oomen et al. (2021, p. 11).

Oomen and colleagues asked all autistic adults 'What changes, due to the effects of the COVID-19 regulations on your everyday life, have caused the most stress/anxiety (if any)?' In response, some explained that the COVID-19 pandemic has had a profound impact on their ability to do shopping for two reasons. First, their shopping activities were disrupted by the COVID-19 pandemic, in particular the unavailability of specific products, limitations on the number of products that could be purchased or time spent in the shop, and having to line up and wait to enter into a shop. Second, due to social distancing regulations shopping was considered more stressful. For example, some found it difficult to adhere to the rules imposed when going shopping while others had anxiety when they saw others not adhering to the rules. The thought of having to change their routines and return to their previous 'normal' life after the COVID-19 pandemic was another anxiety-provoking factor. For example, some were concerned about being exposed to noisy environments, such as traffic and the noise generated by crowds after the lockdown ended (Oomen et al., 2021) (see Table 3.13).

Table 3.13. Themes Identified from Responses of Autistic Adults to the Following Open Question: What Changes, Due to the Effects of the COVID-19 Regulations on Your Everyday Life, Have Caused the Most Stress/Anxiety (If Any)?

Theme	Subtheme	Example Quote
Groceries	Disrupted shopping routines	'The unavailability of my specific groceries, for weeks now. Getting to the shop and seeing empty shelves, yet again, bring me to tears. Because it's something I have absolutely no control over. And having to change what I eat on top of everything else is just too much'. p. 611
		'Unable to do groceries due to meltdowns/or panic attacks not sure which of these is the culprit. Sensory overload is entangled with supermarkets on a regular day, with all the change it's become impossible to do on my own'. p. 440
		'Shopping—not being able to get my routine food'. p. 86
	Social distancing rules	'Not being able to go grocery shopping without a lot of anxiety. I only go once a week, whereas I was used to go almost daily. I am very scared about people at the shops not adhering to the rules'. p. 432
		'Grocery shopping is awful now! It was always awful to begin with, but with all the extra regulations it's even more stressful now. Constantly having to keep my distance and reminding myself is an extra, unwanted step in this already exhausting process of having to do everything right, having to think of everything. I now come home upset and sweaty every time'. p. 442

Table 3.13. *(Continued)*

Theme	Subtheme	Example Quote
Going back to normal		'The sudden change in my routine and then the sudden change in going back to my previous routine when this has ended. My threshold for external stimulus is non-existence now so I am fearful that, when I do return to work, I am going to be exhausted due to sensory overload on my commute to/from work and the social interaction is going to also be exhausting. I am not "masking" anymore and I am concerned I will have forgotten how to do that and how to hide my stimming. The reality is it is probably muscle memory at this point in my life but the exhaustion from external stimuli is worrying me'. p. 977 'The relief of not having to mask anymore, but simultaneously the worry I will not be able to join back the rat race as quickly as the others. When things will open back up, expectations of enjoying the social get together will be super high and I will be enormously stressed and out of practice in acting normal'. p. 579 'After a few weeks I have now gotten used to this calm pace, these new social rules slowly seem clear to me, so now it gives me a little anxiety that afterwards I will have to get used to the hustle and bustle and chaos again, and having to find my own way in this'. [Translated] p. 317

Source: Oomen et al. (2021, p. 12).

Oomen and colleagues also asked all autistic participants what aspects of the COVID-19 pandemic had made their lives easier and more enjoyable. Most of their answers were coded under the main theme of an 'autism friendly world'. Under this main theme two subthemes were identified; 'social cohesion/solidarity' and 'reduced sensory and social overload'. Regarding 'social cohesion/solidarity' many claimed that during lockdowns many non-autistic adults were living a socially isolated lifestyle that was like the way in which they lived their lives. For example, some explained that when non-autistic adults had to isolate themselves to avoid contracting the SARS-CoV-2 virus this was like them isolating themselves so that they did not encounter sensory overload. For some autistic adults this realisation created a feeling of solidarity towards their non-autistic counterparts. Regarding 'reduced sensory and social overload' several autistic participants explained that lockdown situations created less sensory stimulating environments which made them feel relaxed. Similarly, during lockdowns autistic adults felt a sense of ease because they did not need to attend social appointments, accept unplanned invitations to social events from others, nor continually experience strangers getting physically close (Oomen et al., 2021).

Oomen and colleagues also reported that both autistic and non-autistic adults explained that they enjoyed having time to amuse themselves during lockdown. Autistic adults especially enjoyed this experience since it allowed them the opportunity to indulge in their passions and interests. Additionally, both autistic and non-autistic adults also enjoyed having complete control of their daily activities (e.g. when to take a break from work), having the option to work from home for a few months, and the overall pressure of adhering to societal expectations of everyday life being diminished (Oomen et al., 2021) (see Table 3.14).

Table 3.14. Themes Identified from Autistic Adults' Responses to the Following Open Question: What Changes, Due to the Effects of the COVID-19 Regulations on Your Everyday Life, Have Made Life More Pleasant for You (If Any)?

Theme	Subtheme	Example Quote
Autism-friendly world	Social cohesion/ solidarity	'As the entire nation is on lockdown, and everyone is self-isolating, I feel like I am finally at one with society. My way of living life is the norm. I no longer have to feel alone. I have a sense of belonging that everyone is in the same situation and we're all in this together'. p. 629 'I notice that I find the contact with friends and my parents more pleasant now: I feel like my own and their daily worlds have more of a common denominator now. There's a difficult situation now, that others also intuitively experience as being difficult. (. . .) Furthermore, interactions are more frequent but shorter, maybe that's why I feel less like I have to dig into my reserves in order to lead the social life that I want'. [Translated] p. 668
	Reduced sensory and social overload	'These times are in many respects more autism-friendly. There's less car traffic and noise in

Table 3.14. *(Continued)*

Theme	Subtheme	Example Quote
		my neighbourhood. There's less traffic jam frustration and fewer exhaust gases. Working from home is a nice experiment that the crisis made possible. It is less stressful, because I am not disturbed and distracted by colleagues. And because I can take breaks whenever I need it, without worrying about social control. And the stress from socially obligated small talk is no longer there'. [Translated] p. 505
		'No more handshaking, no more people getting way too close and not feeling weird for staying at home all the time'. p. 233

Source: Oomen et al. (2021, p. 12).

3.3.3 Studies with Mixed Samples of Autistic Children and Adults

Of the two studies that contained a mixed sample of autistic children and adults, one was conducted in Spain (Lugo-Marín et al., 2021) while the other was conducted in Turkey (Mutluer et al., 2020). Lugo-Marín et al.'s (2021) study had the smallest sample of autistic participants while Mutluer et al.'s (2020) study had the largest sample. Both studies collected data via surveys (see Table 3.15). What follows now is a description of each study's aims, methods of data collection and results.

Table 3.15. Studies that Contain Mixed Samples of Autistic Children and Adults.

Study	Location of Participants	No. of Autistic Participants	Data Collection Method
Lugo-Marín et al. (2021)	Spain*	children/adolescents = 37 (86.5% male, 13.5% female) adults = 35 (65.7% male, 34.3% female)	Survey
Mutluer et al. (2020)	Turkey	87 (72 male, 14 female)	Survey

Key: * Location of first author since location of participants was not stated in the study.

Lugo-Marín and colleagues examined the psychological impacts that COVID-19 lockdowns had on autistic children or adolescents and autistic adults. All participants complete a 10-point Likert scale survey that measured seven aspects of functioning for autistics. These seven aspects were: mood/irritability, sleep quality, feeding quality, weight, number of social interactions, anxiety and internalising/externalising behaviours. Depending on the question, the possible response options were either 'worse, less, or low', 'no change' or 'better, more, or high'. The results showed that during the onset of the lockdown autistic adults experienced a decrease in stress levels while caregivers reported that their autistic children had higher levels of stress during this time.

In Mutluer et al.'s (2020) study 97 parents of autistic children completed a series of questionnaires. The data collected showed that parents believed that their autistic children did not understand the COVID-19 pandemic (n = 49, 58%) or related pandemic measures and necessities such as staying home or social distancing (n = 40, 47%) (see Table 3.16).

Table 3.16. Parent-Reported Information of COVID-19 Related Understanding and Problems for Autistic Children and Adolescents.

Question	Response	Frequency (%), Number (*n*)
Are there any individuals in your family being treated for COVID-19?	Yes	2% (2)
	No	98% (85)
Is your child's special education continuing during the COVID-19 process?	Yes	8% (78)
	No	92% (78)
How well did your child understand what COVID-19 is?	Not much	58% (49)
	Medium	21% (19)
	Well	20% (17)
How well did your child understand COVID-19-related measures and necessities such as staying home and social distancing?	Not much	47% (40)
	Medium	28% (24)
	Well	24% (20)
Is your child able to follow COVID-19 measures (staying at home, keeping social distance etc.)?	Yes	55% (46)
	No	45% (37)
Can your child perform measures such as washing hands, wearing masks and gloves, and using disinfectants under your instruction?	Yes	80% (66)
	No	20% (17)

Table 3.16. *(Continued)*

Question	Response	Frequency (%), Number (*n*)
Is your child experiencing sensory problems while implementing these measures of wearing masks and gloves, washing hands, and using disinfectants?	Yes	37% (31)
	No	63% (52)
Do you use a resource explaining what COVID-19 is and what needs to be done?	Yes	20% (17)
	No	80% (66)
If you are not using it, would you want such a resource for children with ASD, and if it existed, would you use it?	Yes	85% (56)
	No	15% (10)
Is your child using online, remote conference media such as Zoom, Teams etc.?	Yes	29% (24)
	No	71% (60)

Source: Mutluer et al. (2020, p. 6).

Parents also completed the *Aberrant Behaviour Checklist* (ABC) on behalf of their autistic children before and during the COVID-19 pandemic. Their responses showed that during this pandemic their autistic children had elevated levels for all ABC subscales. Parents also reported that their autistic children had increased sleep problems and sensory hypersensitivity disruptions during the COVID-19 pandemic than before this pandemic (Mutluer et al., 2020) (see Table 3.17).

Table 3.17. Behaviour, Sleep Quality, and Hypersensitivity Differences before and during the COVID-19 Pandemic.

Variable	Before the Pandemic Mean ± SD	During the Pandemic Mean ± SD	*t*	*p*	Cohen's d
ABC Total Score	48.4 ± 24.6	57.6 ± 27.7			
ABC subscales					
Irritability	12.6 ± 8.1	15.4 ± 9.4	5.3	0.000	0.57
Lethargy/social withdrawal	10.0 ± 5.9	11.8 ± 8.2	3.5	0.001	0.37
Stereotypical behaviour	6.2 ± 4.1	7.3 ± 4.6	4.5	0.000	0.49

Table 3.17. *(Continued)*

Variable	Before the Pandemic Mean ± SD	During the Pandemic Mean ± SD	*t*	*p*	Cohen's d
Hyperactivity	15.9 ± 9.2	18.6 ± 10.3	4.9	0.000	0.54
Inappropriate speech	3.3 ± 2.9	3.9 ± 3.4	3.8	0.000	0.41
Self-injury	1.2 ± 1.8	1.4 ± 2.0	2.0	0.054	0.22
Sleep-related problems					
Sleep latency	2.3 ± 1.2	2.4 ± 1.2	0.7	0.465	0.08
Sleep disturbance	2.5 ± 1.1	2.8 ± 1.2	2.7	0.010	0.26
Sleep duration (hours)	8.2 ± 2.0	7.6 ± 2.4	− 3.0	0.004	0.26
Sleep quality	2.1 ± 0.8	2.2 ± 0.8	2.1	0.040	0.27
Sensory hypersensitivity	2.7 ± 1.2	2.9 ± 1.2	2.5	0.015	0.17

Key: ABC = Aberrant Behaviour Checklist.

Source: Mutluer et al. (2020, p. 6).

3.4 GAPS IN THE EXISTING LITERATURE

3.4.1 Parents Raising Autistic Children

The limitations of the five studies about parents raising autistic children during the COVID-19 pandemic can provide suggestions for conducting research in the future. Most studies reported that their samples were in some form homogeneous. For example, most parents in Alhuzimi's (2021) study were from affluent backgrounds. Thus, the experiences of parents from less-affluent backgrounds were not captured. Parents in Althiabi's (2021) and Alhuzimi's studies lived in metropolitan regions in the Kingdom of Saudi Arabia. Therefore, their results cannot be generalised to other countries or rural areas in the Kingdom of Saudi Arabia. Similarly, parents who participated in Manning et al. (2021) study lived in Michigan. Since they lived in one area it was not possible to generalise the results to parents who lived in other countries or different areas in the United States. In Tokatly Latzer et al.'s (2021) study, not many fathers participated (n = 6, 19%) relative to mothers (n = 25, 81%). Consequently, it is difficult for the results discovered to be generalised to fathers raising autistic children (see Table 3.18).

Table 3.18. Limitations of Studies about Parents Raising Autistic Children.

	Limitations		
Study	**Homogeneous Sample**	**Methodological Flaws**	**Small Number of Participants**
Alhuzimi (2021)	X		
Althiabi (2021)	X		
Manning et al. (2021)	X	X	
Tokatly Latzer et al. (2021)	X	X	X
Wang et al. (2021)		X	

Key: X = Limitation in the study.

Three studies cited methodological flaws that could hamper the validity of the results reported. Manning and colleagues explained that the autistic children's level of support needs were reported by their parents and not confirmed by diagnostic instruments. Tokatly Latzer and colleagues reported that despite their intention for their open-ended interview questions to evoke detailed qualitative answers, some participants only provided succinct responses. Finally, for Wang et al.'s (2021) study participants were not randomly sampled because they were recruited via convenience sampling. Thus, the results could not be generalised (see Table 3.18).

A small number of participants can often undermine the ability to generalise the results collected to an entire population. Tokatly Latzer and colleagues explained that their results were based on 31 parents (six male, 25 female) who were all recruited from one area in Israel. Consequently, it is difficult, if not impossible, to apply their results to other parents raising autistic children either in Israel or internationally (see Table 3.18).

In the future, researchers could address these limitations by adopting two recommendations. First, they can make their samples more heterogeneous by recruiting parents from different backgrounds, regions and countries. Additionally, they could also include grandparents raising their autistic grandchildren. Second, they can use a variety of approaches to obtaining data from parents and caregivers, such as interviews, surveys and focus groups. If studies conducted in the future adopted these two recommendations, then our understanding of parents and grandparents raising autistic children during the ongoing COVID-19 pandemic could improve.

3.4.2 Experiences of Autistic Adults During the COVID-19 Pandemic

Four of the five (80%) studies about autistic adults and their experiences of the COVID-19 pandemic claimed that their samples were in some form homogeneous. Consequently, the results obtained do not represent the wider population of autistic adults during the COVID-19 pandemic. Bal et al. (2021) claimed that their sample was not ethnically diverse because 87.4% of their participants were white. Additionally, two-thirds of their sample (*n* = 263) reported being employed (full-time = 34.8%, part-time = 22%, self-employed/others = 9.6%). Due to these sample characteristics their result might not be applicable to autistics who are non-white and/or those who are unemployed. Goldfarb et al. (2022) derived their results from a sample that had a large proportion of employees who worked in the field of computer and information technology. The impacts of the COVID-19 pandemic on these industries may be different from other industries. For example, unlike other professions, since many tasks in information technology can be completed from home, such professionals adhere to the health authority's social distancing requirements. Hence, the results collected cannot be generalised to the entire workforce of autistics. Respondents in Oomen et al. (2021) study resided in Belgium (*n* = 517, 49.5), the Netherlands (*n* = 244, 23.4%) and the United Kingdom (*n* = 283, 27.1%). Since most respondents lived in Belgium the results reported may not be entirely representative of those who lived in the Netherlands or the United Kingdom. Pfeiffer et al. (2022) cautioned that their results need to be treated with caution since the sample size was only six participants all recruited from a single country (see Table 3.19). In the future, if studies contained

Table 3.19. Limitations of Studies about Autistic Adults During the COVID-19 Pandemic.

	Limitations	
Study	**Homogeneous Sample**	**Methodological Flaws**
Adams et al. (2021)		X
Bal et al. (2021)	X	
Goldfarb et al. (2022)	X	
Oomen et al. (2021)	X	
Pfeiffer et al. (2022)	X	

Key: X = Limitation in the study.

heterogeneous samples, then they could be more methodologically rigorous than those reviewed in this section.

Adams et al. (2021) cited two methodological flaws in their study. First, their study did not have a control group that could have been used to compare autistics and non-autistics and their experiences of the COVID-19 pandemic. Second, they claimed that a more comprehensive measure of stress could have been used to determine the mental anguish autistics have experienced during the COVID-19 pandemic (see Table 3.19). If scholars produced studies that addressed these two methodological shortcomings, then the results yielded could more accurately describe the experiences of autistic adults during the COVID-19 pandemic.

3.4.3 Experiences of Autistic Children During the COVID-19 Pandemic

Five of the nine (55.55%) studies about autistic children and their experiences of the COVID-19 pandemic contained small samples of autistic children or parents of autistic children (Corbett et al., 2021; Garcia et al., 2021; Kawabe et al., 2020; Mumbardó-Adam et al., 2021; Türkoğlu et al., 2020). For example, Garcia et al.'s (2021) study contained nine participants, Mumbardó-Adam et al.'s (2021) study contained 47 participants and Türkoğlu et al.'s (2020) study contained 46 participants. Due to the small number of participants sampled it is extremely difficult to generalise the results obtained to the entire autistic population (see Table 3.20). To overcome this limitation, in the future researchers should conduct studies that have larger numbers of participants.

Three of the eight (37.5%) studies about autistic children and their experiences of the COVID-19 pandemic reported that their samples were in some form homogeneous. Berard et al. (2021) stated that all the autistic participants in their study had high scores regarding cognitive adaptive levels. Consequently, their results are not representative of the wider autistic population. Corbett et al. (2021) stated that their sample was homogeneous because participants were predominantly white (84.42%), from middle to upper-middle income families, and from one region in the United States. Similarly, all children in Kawabe et al.'s (2020) study resided in the Ehime prefecture, an island in Japan in which people predominantly live rurally. Thus, it may not be possible to generalise the results collected to other areas of Japan. Incorporating participants from more diverse backgrounds into the sample would create more heterogeneous samples that could make the results more representative of the autistic population (see Table 3.20).

Table 3.20. Limitations of Studies about Autistic Children during the COVID-19 Pandemic.

Study	Limitations		
	Small Number of Participants	Homogeneous Sample	Methodological Flaws
Berard et al. (2021)		X	X
Colizzi et al. (2020)			X
Corbett et al. (2021)	X	X	
Garcia et al. (2021)	X		X
Huang et al. (2021)			X
Kawabe et al. (2020)	X	X	X
Mumbardó-Adam et al. (2021)	X		X
Türkoğlu et al. (2020)	X		

Key: X = Limitation in the study.

Six of the nine (66.66%) studies about autistic children and their experiences of the COVID-19 pandemic cited methodological flaws. For Berard et al.'s (2021) study, most of the questionnaires were completed by only one parent (86.2%). Consequently, differing views between parents about their autistic child's experiences of the COVID-19 pandemic were not captured. The survey that Colizzi et al. (2020) used did not contain any standardised assessments of clinical features. This shortcoming meant that it was not possible to compare results between their study and others. Garcia et al. (2021) stated that they used self-reported questionnaires to collect data from participants. Such data collection instruments may be prone to bias, especially when participants are motivated to produce answers that they think would be appealing to the researcher. Huang et al. (2021) used a survey that did not capture data about the autistic child's level of support needs or their co-morbidities. Not collecting these details has meant that researchers were unable to compare the results of their study to others published about this topic. Similarly, Mumbardó-Adam et al.'s (2021) study did not collect information about the family's socioeconomic background nor the autistic child's social and communicative abilities or repetitive behaviours. Likewise, due to ethical concerns regarding confidentiality and anonymity, Kawabe et al. (2020) did not collect data about the educational background of the mothers who participated in their study (see Table 3.20). By addressing these limitations, the results collected would be more representative of the experiences of parents raising autistic children during the COVID-19 pandemic.

3.5 TOPICS THAT HAVE NOT BEEN RESEARCHED

3.5.1 Vaccine Hesitancy Among Autistics

The influence of a person's circumstances, characteristics and beliefs about vaccine safety on their willingness to be vaccinated against COVID-19 has been examined (Fisher et al., 2020; Kreps et al., 2020; Reiter et al., 2020; Robertson et al., 2021; Robinson et al., 2021; Sallam, 2021; Troiano & Nardi, 2021). Edwards et al. (2021) collected from 3000 adults who lived in Australia their demographic characteristics and their political and social attitudes to determine if these factors had an impact on their level of resistance to accepting a vaccine that prevented or mitigated illness from COVID-19. They reported that people were more inclined to refuse this vaccine if they were female, lived in a poor area, downplayed the risks of COVID-19 disease, or held populist political views or devout religious convictions. In contrast, those who lived in households that had high incomes, who were willing to socially distance themselves from others, who used the COVID-safe App to track their location, or who supported the government's policies were more inclined to be vaccinated against COVID-19 disease.

The reluctance among healthcare workers to get vaccinated against COVID-19 disease has been the focus of many studies (Kwok et al., 2021). For their scoping review, Biswas et al. (2021) reviewed 35 studies about COVID-19 vaccine hesitancy among healthcare workers. They calculated that across the world the proportion of healthcare workers who were hesitant to the COVID-19 vaccine ranged from 4.3 to 72%, with the average being 22.51%. According to most studies, the main reasons for COVID-19 vaccine hesitancy were concerns about vaccine safety, efficacy and potential side effects. Additionally, most studies reported that COVID-19 vaccine uptake was the greatest amongst those who were male, of older age, holders of doctoral degrees, who held a higher perceived risk of getting infected with COVID-19 and a history of getting influenza vaccinations.

Unlike the plethora of research about the reasons for vaccine hesitancy among the non-autistic population, there is an absence of literature about possible vaccine hesitancy among autistics and their families. It is possible that the production of research about this topic could be inhibited because some researchers are concerned about the continuing scandal around the fraudulent research that Wakefield and colleagues published about vaccines and autism (Burgess et al., 2006). It is possible that more non-autistic families might harbour the misleading belief that vaccines are a contributing factor to the development of autism (Bennett et al., 2018). To correct this imbalance, the online survey distributed to autistics in this study aimed to capture the insights from autistics and their families about vaccine hesitancy.

3.5.2 Conducting More Research About Autistic Adults and Their Experiences of the COVID-19 Pandemic

The PRISMA analysis process revealed that there were nine studies about parents describing their autistic child's experiences of the COVID-19 pandemic (Berard et al., 2021; Colizzi et al., 2020; Corbett et al., 2021; Garcia et al., 2021; Huang et al., 2021; Kawabe et al., 2020; Mumbardó-Adam et al., 2021; Nuñez et al., 2021; Türkoğlu et al., 2020) and five studies about autistic adults describing their experiences of this pandemic (Adams et al., 2021; Bal et al., 2021; Goldfarb et al., 2022; Oomen et al., 2021; Pfeiffer et al., 2022). Based on this imbalance of research, it would be prudent to conduct more research about autistic adults and their experiences of the COVID-19 pandemic. Additionally, except for Goldfarb et al.'s (2022) study, all other studies about adults describing their experiences of the COVID-19 pandemic obtained their data via surveys. In the future, more studies should follow Goldfarb et al.'s approach and use a combination of surveys and interviews to collect views from autistic adults. To address this gap in our knowledge the online survey used in this study had a combination of closed questions and free-text responses to obtain data from autistic adults about their experiences of the COVID-19 pandemic.

3.5.3 Conducting More Research About Autistic Adults with COVID-19 Disease

There are several studies about the experiences of patients with COVID-19 disease, including a relatively unexplored condition that has been termed 'long COVID', which refers to having COVID-19 symptoms after the initial infection has ended (Iqbal et al., 2021; Kingstone et al., 2020; Taylor et al., 2021). In contrast, no studies were located that contained descriptions of autistic adults describing what it is like to have COVID-19 disease. In the future, studies should address this gap, including whether these individuals have then gone on to experience 'long COVID'. The consequence of exploring this topic is that healthcare professionals would have a better understanding about the challenges that autistic adults encounter with COVID-19 disease and a more comprehensive understanding about the suitable treatment and support strategies to help them during and after this disease. The online survey in this study addressed this gap in our knowledge by asking autistic participants about their experiences of COVID-19 disease.

3.6 CONCLUSION

This chapter furnished the reader with an overview of the results from the PRISMA analysis process that helped to identify the literature about autistics and parents of autistics and their experiences of the COVID-19 pandemic. Three gaps in our knowledge about this topic were then outlined, which were vaccine hesitancy among autistics and parents raising autistic children, the experiences of autistics living with COVID-19 disease and parenting an autistic child during the COVID-19 pandemic. To help address these three gaps an online survey was completed by autistics and parents of autistics. The next chapter outlines the results from this online survey.

REFERENCES

Adams, R. E., Zheng, S., Taylor, J. L., & Bishop, S. L. (2021). Ten weeks in: COVID-19-related distress in adults with autism spectrum disorder. *Autism: The International Journal of Research and Practice*, *25*(7), 2140–2145. https://doi.org/10.1177/13623613211005919

Alhuzimi, T. (2021). Stress and emotional wellbeing of parents due to change in routine for children with Autism Spectrum Disorder (ASD) at home during COVID-19 pandemic in Saudi Arabia. *Research in Developmental Disabilities*, *108*, 103822. https://doi.org/10.1016/j.ridd.2020.103822

Althiabi, Y. (2021). Attitude, anxiety and perceived mental health care needs among parents of children with Autism Spectrum Disorder (ASD) in Saudi Arabia during COVID-19 pandemic. *Research in Developmental Disabilities*, *111*, 103873. https://doi.org/10.1016/j.ridd.2021.103873

Bal, V. H., Wilkinson, E., White, L. C., Law, J. K., SPARK Consortium, Feliciano, P., & Chung, W. K. (2021). Early pandemic experiences of autistic adults: Predictors of psychological distress. *Autism Research: Official Journal of the International Society for Autism Research*, *14*(6), 1209–1219. https://doi.org/10.1002/aur.2480

Bennett, M., Webster, A. A., Goodall, E., & Rowland, S. (2018). Challenging the public's perception of life on autism spectrum: The impact of the vaccination myth. In *Life on the autism spectrum* (pp. 37–60). Springer. https://doi.org/10.1007/978-981-13-3359-0_3

Berard, M., Rattaz, C., Peries, M., Loubersac, J., Munir, K., & Baghdadli, A. (2021). Impact of containment and mitigation measures on children and youth with ASD during the COVID-19 pandemic: Report from the ELENA cohort. *Journal of Psychiatric Research*, *137*, 73–80. https://doi.org/10.1016/j.jpsychires.2021.02.041

Biswas, N., Mustapha, T., Khubchandani, J., & Price, J. H. (2021). The nature and extent of COVID-19 vaccination hesitancy in healthcare workers. *Journal of Community Health*, *46*(6), 1244–1251. https://doi.org/10.1007/s10900-021-00984-3

Burgess, D. C., Burgess, M. A., & Leask, J. (2006). The MMR vaccination and autism controversy in United Kingdom 1998–2005: Inevitable community outrage or a failure of risk communication? *Vaccine*, *24*(18), 3921–3928. https://doi.org/10.1016/j.vaccine.2006.02.033

Colizzi, M., Sironi, E., Antonini, F., Ciceri, M. L., Bovo, C., & Zoccante, L. (2020). Psychosocial and behavioral impact of COVID-19 in autism spectrum disorder: An online parent survey. *Brain Sciences*, *10*(6), 341. https://doi.org/10.3390/brainsci10060341

Corbett, B. A., Muscatello, R. A., Klemencic, M. E., & Schwartzman, J. M. (2021). The impact of COVID-19 on stress, anxiety, and coping in youth with and without autism and their parents. *Autism Research: Official Journal of the International Society for Autism Research*, *14*(7), 1496–1511. https://doi.org/10.1002/aur.2521

Edwards, B., Biddle, N., Gray, M., & Sollis, K. (2021). COVID-19 vaccine hesitancy and resistance: Correlates in a nationally representative longitudinal survey of the Australian population. *PLoS One*, *16*(3), e0248892. https://doi.org/10.1371/journal.pone.0248892

Fisher, K. A., Bloomstone, S. J., Walder, J., Crawford, S., Fouayzi, H., & Mazor, K. M. (2020). Attitudes toward a potential SARS-CoV-2 vaccine: A survey of US adults. *Annals of Internal Medicine, 173*(12), 964–973. https://doi.org/10.7326/M20-3569

Garcia, J. M., Lawrence, S., Brazendale, K., Leahy, N., & Fukuda, D. (2021). Brief report: The impact of the COVID-19 pandemic on health behaviors in adolescents with autism spectrum disorder. *Disability and Health Journal, 14*(2), 101021. https://doi.org/10.1016/j.dhjo.2020.101021

Goldfarb, Y., Gal, E., & Golan, O. (2022). Implications of employment changes caused by COVID-19 on mental health and work-related psychological need satisfaction of autistic employees: A mixed-methods longitudinal study. *Journal of Autism and Developmental Disorders, 52*(1), 89–102. https://doi.org/10.1007/s10803-021-04902-3

Huang, S., Sun, T., Zhu, Y., Song, S., Zhang, J., Huang, L., Chen, Q., Peng, G., Zhao, D., Yu, H., & Jing, J. (2021). Impact of the COVID-19 pandemic on children with ASD and their families: An online survey in China. *Psychology Research and Behavior Management, 14*, 289–297. https://doi.org/10.2147/PRBM.S293426

Iqbal, F. M., Lam, K., Sounderajah, V., Clarke, J. M., Ashrafian, H., & Darzi, A. (2021). Characteristics and predictors of acute and chronic post-COVID syndrome: A systematic review and meta-analysis. *EClinicalMedicine, 36*, 100899. https://doi.org/10.1016/j.eclinm.2021.100899

Kawabe, K., Hosokawa, R., Nakachi, K., Yoshino, A., Horiuchi, F., & Ueno, S. I. (2020). Excessive and problematic internet use during the Coronavirus disease 2019 school closure: Comparison between Japanese youth with and without autism spectrum disorder. *Frontiers in Public Health, 8*, 609347. https://doi.org/10.3389/fpubh.2020.609347

Kingstone, T., Taylor, A. K., O'Donnell, C. A., Atherton, H., Blane, D. N., & Chew-Graham, C. A. (2020). Finding the 'right' GP: A qualitative study of the experiences of people with long-COVID. *BJGP Open, 4*(5). https://doi.org/10.3399/bjgpopen20X101143

Kreps, S., Prasad, S., Brownstein, J. S., Hswen, Y., Garibaldi, B. T., Zhang, B., & Kriner, D. L. (2020). Factors associated with US adults' likelihood of accepting COVID-19 vaccination. *JAMA Network Open, 3*(10), e2025594. https://doi.org/10.1001/jamanetworkopen.2020.25594

Kwok, K. O., Li, K. K., Wei, W. I., Tang, A., Wong, S., & Lee, S. S. (2021). Editor's Choice: Influenza vaccine uptake, COVID-19 vaccination intention and vaccine hesitancy among nurses: A survey. *International Journal of Nursing Studies*, *114*, 103854. https://doi.org/10.1016/j.ijnurstu.2020.103854

Lugo-Marín, J., Gisbert-Gustemps, L., Setien-Ramos, I., Español-Martín, G., Ibañez-Jimenez, P., Forner-Puntonet, M., Arteaga-Henríquez, G., Soriano-Día, A., Duque-Yemail, J. D., & Ramos-Quiroga, J. A. (2021). COVID-19 pandemic effects in people with Autism Spectrum Disorder and their caregivers: Evaluation of social distancing and lockdown impact on mental health and general status. *Research in Autism Spectrum Disorders*, *83*, 101757. https://doi.org/10.1016/j.rasd.2021.101757

Manning, J., Billian, J., Matson, J., Allen, C., & Soares, N. (2021). Perceptions of families of individuals with autism spectrum disorder during the COVID-19 Crisis. *Journal of Autism and Developmental Disorders*, *51*(8), 2920–2928. https://doi.org/10.1007/s10803-020-04760-5

Mumbardó-Adam, C., Barnet-López, S., & Balboni, G. (2021). How have youth with autism spectrum disorder managed quarantine derived from COVID-19 pandemic? An approach to families perspectives. *Research in Developmental Disabilities*, *110*, 103860. https://doi.org/10.1016/j.ridd.2021.103860

Mutluer, T., Doenyas, C., & Aslan Genc, H. (2020). Behavioral implications of the Covid-19 process for autism spectrum disorder, and individuals' comprehension of and reactions to the pandemic conditions. *Frontiers in Psychiatry*, *11*, 561882. https://doi.org/10.3389/fpsyt.2020.561882

Nuñez, A., Le Roy, C., Coelho-Medeiros, M. E., & López-Espejo, M. (2021). Factors affecting the behavior of children with ASD during the first outbreak of the COVID-19 pandemic. *Neurological Sciences: Official Journal of the Italian Neurological Society and of the Italian Society of Clinical Neurophysiology*, *42*(5), 1675–1678. https://doi.org/10.1007/s10072-021-05147-9

Oomen, D., Nijhof, A. D., & Wiersema, J. R. (2021). The psychological impact of the COVID-19 pandemic on adults with autism: A survey study across three countries. *Molecular Autism*, *12*(1), 21. https://doi.org/10.1186/s13229-021-00424-y

Pfeiffer, B., Brusilovskiy, E., Hallock, T., Salzer, M., Davidson, A. P., Slugg, L., & Feeley, C. (2022). Impact of COVID-19 on community participation and mobility in young adults with autism spectrum disorders. *Journal of Autism and Developmental Disorders*, *52*(4), 1553–1567. https://doi.org/10.1007/s10803-021-05054-0

Reiter, P. L., Pennell, M. L., & Katz, M. L. (2020). Acceptability of a COVID-19 vaccine among adults in the United States: How many people would get vaccinated? *Vaccine*, *38*(42), 6500–6507. https://doi.org/10.1016/j.vaccine.2020.08.043

Robertson, E., Reeve, K. S., Niedzwiedz, C. L., Moore, J., Blake, M., Green, M., Katikireddi, S. V., & Benzeval, M. J. (2021). Predictors of COVID-19 vaccine hesitancy in the UK household longitudinal study. *Brain, Behavior, and Immunity, 94*, 41–50. https://doi.org/10.1016/j.bbi.2021.03.008

Robinson, E., Jones, A., Lesser, I., & Daly, M. (2021). International estimates of intended uptake and refusal of COVID-19 vaccines: A rapid systematic review and meta-analysis of large nationally representative samples. *Vaccine, 39*(15), 2024–2034. https://doi.org/10.1016/j.vaccine.2021.02.005

Sallam, M. (2021). COVID-19 vaccine hesitancy worldwide: A concise systematic review of vaccine acceptance rates. *Vaccines*, *9*(2), 160. https://doi.org/10.3390/vaccines9020160

Taylor, A. K., Kingstone, T., Briggs, T. A., O'Donnell, C. A., Atherton, H., Blane, D. N., & Chew-Graham, C. A. (2021). 'Reluctant pioneer': A qualitative study of doctors' experiences as patients with long COVID. *Health Expectations: An International Journal of Public Participation in Health Care and Health Policy*, *24*(3), 833–842. https://doi.org/10.1111/hex.13223

Tokatly Latzer, I., Leitner, Y., & Karnieli-Miller, O. (2021). Core experiences of parents of children with autism during the COVID-19 pandemic lockdown. *Autism: The International Journal of Research and Practice*, *25*(4), 1047–1059. https://doi.org/10.1177/1362361320984317

Troiano, G., & Nardi, A. (2021). Vaccine hesitancy in the era of COVID-19. *Public Health*, *194*, 245–251. https://doi.org/10.1016/j.puhe.2021.02.025

Türkoğlu, S., Uçar, H. N., Çetin, F. H., Güler, H. A., & Tezcan, M. E. (2020). The relationship between chronotype, sleep, and autism symptom severity in children with ASD in COVID-19 home confinement period. *Chronobiology International*, *37*(8), 1207–1213. https://doi.org/10.1080/07420528.2020.1792485

Wang, L., Li, D., Pan, S., Zhai, J., Xia, W., Sun, C., & Zou, M. (2021). The relationship between 2019-nCoV and psychological distress among parents of children with autism spectrum disorder. *Globalization and Health*, *17*(1), 23. https://doi.org/10.1186/s12992-021-00674-8

4

NEW PERSPECTIVES ABOUT THE COVID-19 PANDEMIC FOR AUTISTICS

4.1 INTRODUCTION

In the previous chapter it was revealed that there is a scant amount of literature about the views and experiences of autistics regarding vaccine hesitancy, the COVID-19 pandemic and COVID-19 disease. To address these gaps, an online survey was developed and distributed on two separate occasions to autistics and their families. During its first distribution, it was open for five weeks, from 13 July 2021 to 20 August 2021, and was completed by 32 respondents. During its second distribution it was open for six weeks, from 6 March 2022 to 17 April 2022, and was completed by 34 respondents. In this chapter, a description of the data collected from these two surveys is presented. This is followed by an overview of the benefits and drawbacks associated with using an online survey and the state of the literature about autism and the COVID-19 pandemic after data were collected from the second survey. This chapter then concludes with some final comments about autism and the COVID-19 pandemic.

Keywords: COVID-19 disease; health authorities; online survey; pandemic; social distancing; vaccine hesitancy

4.2 THE ONLINE SURVEY

The scoping review of the literature about autism and the COVID-19 pandemic revealed three topics that have not received much, if any, attention from scholars. These topics were experiences of autistics regarding vaccine hesitancy, the COVID-19 pandemic and COVID-19 disease. To explore these topics, an online survey was developed (see Appendix 2). It was disseminated via three Facebook groups (i.e. Autism parents support group, Autism Family Support Group and Autism Awareness) and via an email that was sent to 100 autistics distributed by the Autism CRC. During its first distribution, it was open for five weeks, from 13 July 2021 to 20 August 2021, and was completed by 32 respondents. During its second distribution, it was open for six weeks, from 6 March 2022 to 17 April 2022, and was completed by 34 respondents. An online survey was used because it was not possible to meet autistics and their parents in person due to social distancing and the limitations associated with physically meeting people. What follows now is a description and analysis of the results from both online surveys.

4.3 SAMPLE CHARACTERISTICS

Before respondents were asked about their perspectives and experiences of the COVID-19 pandemic they were asked to provide their age, gender identity, country of residence and if they had a formal autism diagnosis. Most revealed that they were between 26 and 35 years (n = 23, 34.84%). In contrast, two (3.03%) disclosed that they were aged between 18 and 25 years (see Table 4.1). Most self-identified as cis female (n = 36), followed by those who self-identified as cis male (n = 14) and those who self-identified as gender non-binary (n = 12). Respondents were also asked to state what country they

Table 4.1. Age of Participants.

Age Range	*Survey One* No. of Participants (%)	*Survey Two* No. of Participants (%)	Overall Total (%)
18–25 years	2 (6.25)	0 (0)	**2 (3.03)**
26–35 years	12 (37.50)	11 (32.35)	**23 (34.84)**
36–45 years	9 (28.13)	8 (23.52)	**17 (25.75)**
46–55 years	6 (18.75)	6 (17.64)	**12 (18.18)**
56–65 years	1 (3.13)	5 (14.70)	**6 (9.09)**
65 + years	2 (6.25)	3 (8.82)	**5 (7.57)**
UNKNOWN/NOT STATE	0 (0)	1 (2.94)	**1 (1.51)**
Total	**32 (100%)**	**34 (100%)**	**66 (100%)**

resided in at the time of completing the survey. Most claimed that they lived in the United States of America (n = 18, 27.27%), followed by New Zealand (n = 15, 27.27%), Australia (n = 13, 19.69%) and the United Kingdom (n = 12, 18.18%). Additionally, Canada, China, Germany, the Netherlands and Sweden all had either one respondent or two who completed the online survey (see Table 4.2). Finally, respondents were asked if they had a formal autism diagnosis. Most reported that they did have such a diagnosis (n = 53) and 12 claimed that they self-identified as autistic.

Table 4.2. Country of Residency.

Country of Residency	*Survey One* No. of Participants (%)	*Survey Two* No. of Participants (%)	Overall Total (%)
Australia	7 (21.88)	6 (17.65)	**13 (19.69)**
Canada	1 (3.13)	1 (2.94)	**2 (3.03)**
China	1 (3.13)	0 (0)	**1 (1.51)**
Germany	1 (3.13)	1 (2.94)	**2 (3.03)**
The Netherlands	1 (3.13)	0 (0)	**1 (1.51)**
New Zealand	4 (12.50)	11 (32.35)	**15 (22.72)**
Sweden	1 (3.13)	1 (2.94)	**2 (3.03)**
United Kingdom	5 (15.63)	7 (20.59)	**12 (18.18)**
United States of America	11 (34.38)	7 (20.59)	**18 (27.27)**
Total	**32 (100%)**	**34 (100%)**	**66 (100%)**

4.4 RESTRICTIONS CAUSED BY THE COVID-19 PANDEMIC

Respondents were asked three questions about the restrictions that they may have encountered that were intended to mitigate the detrimental consequences of the COVID-19 pandemic. These three questions were:

- Have you experienced any restrictions that were related to the COVID-19 pandemic? For example, only being able to exercise with one other person, not travelling more than 5 kilometres (3.10 miles) from your home or working from home arrangements.
- What restrictions did you personally experience that were related to the COVID-19 pandemic?

- What techniques and strategies did you use to cope with these restrictions? (You can choose more than one option).

Most stated that they had experienced some form of restriction that was related to the COVID-19 pandemic (n = 61). Respondents were then asked to describe the restrictions that they had personally experienced. Respondents were able to provide more than one answer to this question. Social distancing and wearing a mask in public both received the greatest number of responses (n = 56). In contrast, 24 respondents stated that their 'place of work changed to working from home all or part-time' (see Table 4.3). Finally, participants were asked to explain what techniques and strategies they used to cope with these restrictions. Most revealed that they engaged in their hobbies to maintain their focus and calmness (n = 40). In contrast, three claimed that they took a holiday to cope with the lockdown associated with the COVID-19 pandemic (see Table 4.4).

Table 4.3. Restrictions Related to the COVID-19 Pandemic.

Answer Choices	***Survey One* No. of Responses ***	***Survey Two* No. of Responses ***	**Overall Total**
Lockdown – could not leave home for 3 or more days	11	14	**25**
Lockdown with ability to leave home for limited reasons	21	22	**43**
Lockdown with limited freedom of movement (e.g. 1–5km travel only)	14	17	**31**
Place of work changed to working from home all or part-time	10	14	**24**
Social distancing	27	29	**56**
Mask wearing in public places	27	29	**56**
Other (please specify)	5	12	**17**
Total responses	**115**	**137**	**252**

Selection of other responses for SURVEY ONE were:

(1) Curfew

(2) Children home schooling

(3) Changes and restrictions when accessing medical care, supermarkets, basically everything

(4) Not willing to use public transportation and Uber due to them being enclosed germy environments so just opting to walk

(5) Was unable to work for a period of time; was working in a restaurant

Selection of other responses for SURVEY TWO were:

Table 4.3. *(Continued)*

Answer Choices	***Survey One*** **No. of Responses ***	***Survey Two*** **No. of Responses ***	**Overall Total**

(1) Continuous monitoring of my movements via Bluetooth and a special COVID-19 tracking app – having to register with the government at every store I went to.
(2) A friend had a serious reaction to the vaccine and she was diagnosed with Myocarditis. This made me extremely afraid about the safety of the vaccine. I know that people laugh at me for this fear and call me selfish, but I was terrified. When work mandated the vaccine, I wasn't ready to get it. Unfortunately this meant that I lost my job. I know that this is illogical, but it's taking me a lot of time for me to work on overcoming this fear with a therapist.

Note: * Participants could indicate more than one response.

Table 4.4. Techniques and Strategies Used to Cope with the Restrictions Associated with the COVID-19 Pandemic.

Answer Choices	***Survey One*** **No. of Responses ***	***Survey Two*** **No. of Responses ***	**Overall Total**
I kept in contact with my friends	16	14	**30**
I sought counselling or therapy	5	12	**17**
I sought medical support	4	1	**5**
I engaged in my hobbies to maintain focus and calm	17	23	**40**
I exercised when I could	13	15	**28**
I took a holiday	1	2	**3**
I used non-prescription medication	3	3	**6**
I used prescription medication	10	**7**	**17**
Other (please specify)	8	11	**19**
Total responses	**77**	**88**	**165**

Selection of other responses for SURVEY ONE were:

(1) Used specific recorded music I'd put on iPodto facilitate best recovery ... certain modes that I prefer but also have been shown by research to have positive effect on healing. This helped me to have a relatively restful night even if still unable to sleep. In day watched inane TV shows that I recorded to shut mind down and emotions not disturbing ... superficial series c

Table 4.4. (*Continued*)

Answer Choices	*Survey One* No. of Responses *	*Survey Two* No. of Responses *	Overall Total
(2) I stayed in and avoided doing everything and didn't interact with anybody. I could not cope with the restrictions and changes and there was no support and no accessible info.			
(3) I used my hobbies as a means of staying connected to others			
(4) I moved back in with my parents for a few months during lockdown. I suspended my study (I don't really define this as 'taking a holiday', but would have said it was equivalent to 'taking leave from work')			
(5) Isolated and stopped self-care			
(6) Fantasising			
(7) I didn't have much to cope WITH. I am already primarily housebound.			
(8) I enjoyed solitude and could calm down			
Selection of other responses for SURVEY TWO were:			
(1) Monday to Friday drove to centre to get a bag lunch and talk to staff, lots of zoom meetings, weekly movie night with adult son who lives with me. Talk to husband in nursing home on phone multiple times daily.			

Note: * Participants could indicate more than one response.

4.5 COVID-19 TESTS AND DISEASE

Respondents were asked three questions about taking a COVID-19 test and being diagnosed with COVID-19 disease. These three questions were:

- Have you had one or more COVID-19 tests?
- Have you had or do you have a diagnosis of COVID-19 disease?
- If diagnosed with COVID-19 disease, did you access medical care?

Most claimed that they had received a medical test to diagnose COVID-19 disease (n = 38). However, 27 claimed that they had not taken such a medical test. Respondents were then asked if they had been diagnosed with COVID-19 disease. Most had not been diagnosed with this disease (n = 28) while eight had received such a diagnosis. The eight respondents who had been diagnosed with COVID-19 disease were then asked what medical care they had sought. Two were satisfied with the medical care that they had received and other six respondents claimed that they just self-isolated.

4.6 COVID-19 VACCINE

Respondents were asked four questions about their views and experiences of the COVID-19 vaccines. These four questions were:

- What are your opinions on the COVID-19-19 vaccine?
- Have you already had a COVID-19 vaccine?
- What are your reasons for wanting to be vaccinated against COVID-19 disease? (You can select more than one option).
- What are your reasons for not wanting to be vaccinated?

Most (n = 34) claimed that they were happy to be vaccinated against COVID-19 disease. However, two respondents objected to being vaccinated. Respondents were then asked if they had received a vaccine to prevent the development of COVID-19 disease. Most had received both doses of this vaccine (n = 33), followed by eight who had received one dose of this vaccine, three who had not yet received a COVID-19 vaccine but wanted to receive this vaccine and three who did not intend to be vaccinated against COVID-19 disease. Respondents were then asked to explain their views for wanting to receive a vaccine to protect themselves against the development of COVID-19 disease. Respondents were given the ability to select more than one option. Most (n = 52) claimed that they wanted to take a vaccine so that they could protect themselves from developing COVID-19 disease. In contrast, seven claimed that receiving a vaccine to prevent the development of COVID-19 disease was a requirement of their job (see Table 4.5). Since three respondents did not want to receive the COVID-19 vaccine, they were asked 'What are your reasons for not wanting to be vaccinated?'. In elaborate detail, one respondent revealed the following insights:

> *My initial fear was after a friend had an awful experience & was diagnosed with Myocarditis. This made me wonder about how my body could react. My anxiety escalated unfortunately. It made me wonder about how we can know something is safe without access to any long term studies. I felt really invalidated about my concerns. I'm still actually embarrassed to have those concerns and to not be vaccinated. I want to fit in and I don't want people to think I'm selfish. I also don't want the disease to be a problem in our society. It's just very hard to ignore extreme anxiety about something that left a deep imprint. Any time I tried to be honest about my concerns*

I was called names. I didn't really feel like society were having open conversation about this. It confused me. But maybe I was the only person with questions, concerns or confusion. I've always been weird and stood out for being different, so I guess this is just another situation. I'm still interested in learning more about the new type of vaccine and I'm excited to see the long term studies when that's available. I'm sure by then I'll already have received my vaccines. (Hopefully my anxiety still is not impacting me.) I have received all of my other vaccines. Those ones have been around and I believe there's a lot of evidence to prove it's safety. I believe the COVID-19 vaccines are mostly safe, but still less safe...

Table 4.5. Reasons for Wanting to be Vaccinated Against COVID-19 Disease.

Answer Choices	*Survey One* No. of Responses *	*Survey Two* No. of Responses *	Overall Total
I want to help end the pandemic	23	25	**48**
I want to protect myself against COVID-19 disease	24	28	**52**
I want to protect my family and/or friends against COVID-19 disease	20	29	**49**
I want to be exempt from pandemic-related restrictions	8	4	**12**
I think the benefits outweigh the risks	19	23	**42**
It is a requirement of my job	2	5	**7**
Other (please specify)	4	8	**12**
Total responses	**100**	**122**	**222**

Selection of other responses for SURVEY ONE were:

(1) To piss off the anti-vax people
(2) N/A; see previous response. I find the potential menstruation side effects to be unacceptable.
(3) pretty sure I'd die if I caught it.

Selection of other responses for SURVEY TWO were:

(1) One of my friends died from COVID-19 before vaccines were even available plus I have seen many friends suffer through it (over zoom) before vaccines were available. It seemed like the smart thing to do.
(2) I do not wish to unnecessarily over-burden the healthcare system that is needed for unavoidable illnesses and accidents

Note: * Participants could indicate more than one response.

4.7 PARENTING AN AUTISTIC CHILD DURING THE COVID-19 PANDEMIC

Respondents were then asked seven questions about their experiences about parenting an autistic child during the COVID-19 pandemic. These seven questions were:

- Are you currently raising a child or children on the autism spectrum?
- Has your child on the autism spectrum tested for or been diagnosed with COVID-19?
- Where did you seek help or look for information for your child on the autism spectrum after they were diagnosed with COVID-19 disease? (You can choose more than one option).
- What strategies are you teaching your child on the autism spectrum to protect themselves during the pandemic? (You can choose more than one option).
- Are you intending to get your child on the autism spectrum vaccinated against COVID-19 when they are eligible?
- Why do you intend to get your child/children on the autism spectrum vaccinated?
- Why are you not intending to get your child on the autism spectrum vaccinated?

Most (n = 43) claimed that they were not raising either a child or children on the autism spectrum. However, 20 disclosed that they were parents raising autistic children. Of these 20 respondents, nine did not get their child tested for COVID-19 disease. Additionally, five stated that had their autistic child tested for COVID-19 disease and was found to be a negative result. However, four respondents disclosed that their autistic child tested positive to COVID-19 disease. Respondents were then asked to recall what sources of information and help were accessed to help their autistic child manage their COVID-19 disease. One stated that they had consulted with a medical doctor. Respondents were then asked what strategies they were teaching their autistic child to help them stay safe during the COVID-19 pandemic. One disclosed that they were teaching their autistic child to stay 1.5 metres away from other people, four stated that they were teaching their autistic child to constantly wash their hands and one was teaching their autistic child to wear a face mask. Respondents were then asked if they intended to let their autistic children receive a vaccine that will help them avoid developing COVID-19 disease. In response, 15 claimed that they would let their autistic child receive this vaccine while five replied 'maybe'. Respondents were then asked why they intended to get their autistic child vaccinated against COVID-19 disease. Most (n = 13) replied that they wanted to protect their autistic child against COVID-19 disease. Finally, respondents were asked why they did not intend to get their autistic child vaccinated against COVID-19 disease. Nine answered this question, with two expressing the view that they were concerned that the vaccine would have side-effects, two stated that their autistic child had health issues that would make the vaccine unsafe and five wrote a free-text response. For example, one respondent wrote 'If my child chooses not to get vaccinated, I respect their bodily autonomy'.

4.8 STATE OF THE RESEARCH SINCE THE DISSEMINATION OF THE FIRST ONLINE SURVEY

Since the first online survey closed on 20 August 2021, there has been more research created about autism and the COVID-19 pandemic. To test this proposition, a repeat of the PubMed search was conducted on 27 May 2022, which revealed an additional 191 records along with the original 188 records retrieved from the first search conducted on 4 July 2021. An analysis of these 191 results is documented in Appendix 1 and this analysis showed that 60 citations met the original search criteria. An examination of these citations provided validation to the results generated from the survey. For example, autistics participants who completed the online surveys explained their reasons for obtaining a vaccine to protect them against COVID-19. The findings in Weinstein et al.'s (2021) also echoed their insights. Conversely, new research that was published after the creation of the online survey has provided new insights. For example, the online survey did not ask autistic participants any questions about their mental health or suicide ideation during the COVID-19 pandemic. However, research published after the creation of the online survey revealed that some autistics have experienced depression and/or suicide ideation during the COVID-19 pandemic (Hedley et al., 2021).

4.9 BENEFITS AND DRAWBACKS OF THE ONLINE SURVEY

There are four strengths than the online survey has given this study. First, respondents were not required to reveal their personal details, such as their names. Since they were able to maintain their anonymity, they might have been more willing to provide honest answers. Second, since the online surveys were available to respondents anytime, from 13 July 2021 to 20 August 2021 and from 6 March 2022 to 17 April 2022, they could complete it at a time and place of their convenience. Third, respondents were able to review their answers before they submitted their survey responses. This opportunity enabled them to check their responses for accuracy. Forth, since the survey was delivered online, it was available to a global audience of people who were members of the Facebook groups that the survey link was posted.

Aside from the four benefits mentioned above, there are also five drawbacks from the online survey. First, the respondent was not required to provide any documentation to confirm that they were autistic or that they were parenting an autistic child. Thus, it is possible that the respondents might have falsified their identity. Second, the survey did not provide the opportunity for the views and experiences of respondents to be cross-checked against other people in their lives. Thus, the respondent's accounts might not have been truthful or complete. Third, the online survey was published in English. Thus, some respondents from cultural and linguistically diverse backgrounds would not have had the English language proficiency to successfully complete the online survey. Fourth, the online surveys were distributed to a small group of potential respondents, which resulted in the combined collection of 66 responses. Although the data collected are valuable, they are not in and of themselves representative of the experiences of the entire autistic population or of all parents who are raising autistic children. To ensure that the results can be generalised to these populations, more responses should be collected in the future. Fifth, in the online survey, there was a lack of opportunity to provide free-text responses. With additional studies, it would be advantageous to create a survey that has more opportunities for respondents to write free-text responses or to use a mixed-methods approach of surveys and in-depth interviews to complement the survey responses.

4.10 CLOSING REMARKS

This study had two objectives. First, to present a synthesis of the literature about the impacts of the COVID-19 pandemic from the perspective of autistics and their families and to then highlight any identified gaps in this field of research. Second, to create and then disseminate an online survey to autistics and the parents of autistic children that sought answers to the gaps identified from the literature search. To achieve these two objectives, the following three research questions were posed:

(1) What are the experiences of the COVID-19 pandemic from the perspective of parents raising autistic children?

(2) What impacts has the COVID-19 pandemic had on autistics?

(3) What are the gaps in our understanding about the impact of the COVID-19 pandemic on autistics and their families?

The first literature search of PubMed was conducted on 4 July 2021 and it revealed four main themes. First, during the COVID-19 pandemic, parents raising autistic children often sought advice from other family members, their child's teachers and healthcare professionals (Althiabi, 2021). Second, during this pandemic, they also reported greater rates of anxiety and stress than parents who were raising non-autistic children (Wang et al., 2021). Additionally, parents raising autistic children also described that they had sleeping problems (Huang et al., 2021; Türkoğlu et al., 2020). Third, Huang and colleagues reported that parents of autistic children believed that their social and emotional states became worse during lockdowns. Such emotional difficulties were also confirmed by Nuñez et al. (2021), who reported that in their study 44.9% of parents claimed that when the COVID-19 pandemic started, their autistic children displayed more intense and frequent behavioural problems. Fourth, regarding autistic adults and the COVID-19 pandemic, Bal et al. (2021) reported that those autistics most impacted by the COVID-19 pandemic were female, had a prior diagnosis of a co-morbid health condition and had a personal experience of COVID-19, such as knowing someone who had the symptoms or who tested positive for COVID-19 disease.

Despite the value of the results obtained from the first literature search, they should be endorsed with a degree of caution. An audit of the stated limitations in the studies examined revealed three common shortcomings. First, many based their results on a small number of participants who formed a homogeneous sample. Such samples rendered it difficult, if not impossible, to generalise the results collected to the broader population of autistics and their families. Second, except for two studies (Goldfarb et al., 2022; Tokatly Latzer et al., 2021), all studies reviewed used a survey to obtain data from the participants. Thus, there is a dearth of qualitative data from autistics and their family members. Third, several studies, such as Adams et al.'s (2021) study, did not contain a control group of non-autistics. Thus, it was impossible to fully determine the impact of the ongoing COVID-19 pandemic on autistics since their experiences could not be compared to non-autistics. By addressing these common shortcomings in the published research, along with those that were less common, researchers should be able to provide the academic community with a more accurate understanding of the ongoing COVID-19 pandemic on autistics and their family members.

An appraisal of the collected literature showed that there was a lack of research about vaccine hesitancy among autistics and parents raising autistic children, the experiences of autistics living with COVID-19 disease and parenting an autistic child during the COVID-19 pandemic. To address these gaps, an online survey was designed and disseminated to autistics and those who raise autistic children on two separate occasions (see Appendix 2). These surveys revealed that autistics are generally receptive to receiving a vaccine that will prevent them from developing COVID-19 disease. They also revealed that most autistics engaged in their hobbies to keep calm and relaxed during a lockdown. A second search of the literature on PubMed validated these results. Despite the data collected from the online survey, the results should be treated with caution since they were based on 66 respondents. However, despite this limitation, the online survey can be a template for research in the future about the COVID-19 pandemic and autistics.

REFERENCES

Adams, R. E., Zheng, S., Taylor, J. L., & Bishop, S. L. (2021). Ten weeks in: COVID-19-related distress in adults with autism spectrum disorder. *Autism: The International Journal of Research and Practice*, *25*(7), 2140–2145. https://doi.org/10.1177/13623613211005919

Althiabi, Y. (2021). Attitude, anxiety and perceived mental health care needs among parents of children with Autism Spectrum Disorder (ASD) in Saudi Arabia during COVID-19 pandemic. *Research in Developmental Disabilities*, *111*, 103873. https://doi.org/10.1016/j.ridd.2021.103873

Bal, V. H., Wilkinson, E., White, L. C., Law, J. K., SPARK Consortium, Feliciano, P., & Chung, W. K. (2021). Early pandemic experiences of autistic adults: Predictors of psychological distress. *Autism Research: Official Journal of the International Society for Autism Research*, *14*(6), 1209–1219. https://doi.org/10.1002/aur.2480

Goldfarb, Y., Gal, E., & Golan, O. (2022). Implications of employment changes caused by COVID-19 on mental health and work-related psychological need satisfaction of autistic employees: A mixed-methods longitudinal study. *Journal of Autism and Developmental Disorders*, *52*(1), 89–102. https://doi.org/10.1007/s10803-021-04902-3

Hedley, D., Hayward, S. M., Denney, K., Uljarević, M., Bury, S., Sahin, E., Brown, C. M., Clapperton, A., Dissanayake, C., Robinson, J., Trollor, J., & Stokes, M. A. (2021). The association between COVID-19, personal wellbeing, depression, and suicide risk factors in Australian autistic adults. *Autism Research: Official Journal of the International Society for Autism Research*, *14*(12), 2663–2676. https://doi.org/10.1002/aur.2614

Huang, S., Sun, T., Zhu, Y., Song, S., Zhang, J., Huang, L., Chen, Q., Peng, G., Zhao, D., Yu, H., & Jing, J. (2021). Impact of the COVID-19 pandemic on children with ASD and their families: An online survey in China. *Psychology Research and Behavior Management*, *14*, 289–297. https://doi.org/10.2147/PRBM.S293426

Nuñez, A., Le Roy, C., Coelho-Medeiros, M. E., & López-Espejo, M. (2021). Factors affecting the behavior of children with ASD during the first outbreak of the COVID-19 pandemic. *Neurological Sciences: Official Journal of the Italian Neurological Society and of the Italian Society of Clinical Neurophysiology*, *42*(5), 1675–1678. https://doi.org/10.1007/s10072-021-05147-9

Tokatly Latzer, I., Leitner, Y., & Karnieli-Miller, O. (2021). Core experiences of parents of children with autism during the COVID-19 pandemic lockdown. *Autism: The International Journal of Research and Practice*, *25*(4), 1047–1059. https://doi.org/10.1177/1362361320984317

Türkoğlu, S., Uçar, H. N., Çetin, F. H., Güler, H. A., & Tezcan, M. E. (2020). The relationship between chronotype, sleep, and autism symptom severity in children with ASD in COVID-19 home confinement period. *Chronobiology International*, *37*(8), 1207–1213. https://doi.org/10.1080/07420528.2020.1792485

Wang, L., Li, D., Pan, S., Zhai, J., Xia, W., Sun, C., & Zou, M. (2021). The relationship between 2019-nCoV and psychological distress among parents of children with autism spectrum disorder. *Globalization and Health*, *17*(1), 23. https://doi.org/10.1186/s12992-021-00674-8

Weinstein, O., Krieger, I., Cohen, A. D., & Tzur Bitan, D. (2021). COVID-19 vaccination among individuals with autism spectrum disorder: A population-based study. *Research in Autism Spectrum Disorders*, *89*, 101865. https://doi.org/10.1016/j.rasd.2021.101865

CHOICE OF TERMINOLOGY

There is an ongoing debate in the field of autism spectrum research, as well as in the broader field of disability studies, as to what is the most appropriate use of terminology to address members of the autistic community (Tepest, 2021; Vivanti, 2020). Some people prefer using person-first language (i.e. people on the autism spectrum) while others prefer using identity-first language (i.e. autistic person). Throughout this book we use identity-first language since contemporary research has shown that most autistics prefer this language convention (Bury et al., 2020; Kenny et al., 2016). Furthermore, it is our belief, as autistic researchers, that since the autism spectrum is an inseparable part of a person's identity that the word 'autistic' should be used instead of 'person with autism' or 'person on the autism spectrum'.

REFERENCES

Bury, S. M., Jellett, R., Spoor, J. R., & Hedley, D. (2020). "It defines who I am" or "it's something I have": What language do [autistic] Australian adults [on the autism spectrum] prefer? *Journal of Autism and Developmental Disorders*. https://doi.org/10.1007/s10803-020-04425-3

Kenny, L., Hattersley, C., Molins, B., Buckley, C., Povey, C., & Pellicano, E. (2016). Which terms should be used to describe autism? Perspectives from the UK autism community. *Autism: The International Journal of Research and Practice*, *20*(4), 442–462. https://doi.org/10.1177/1362361315588200

Tepest, R. (2021). The meaning of diagnosis for different designations in talking about autism. *Journal of Autism and Developmental Disorders*, *51*(2), 760–761. https://doi.org/10.1007/s10803-020-04584-3

Vivanti, G. (2020). Ask the editor: What is the most appropriate way to talk about individuals with a diagnosis of autism? *Journal of Autism and Developmental Disorders*, *50*(2), 691–693. https://doi.org/10.1007/s10803-019-04280-x

APPENDICES

APPENDIX 1 – RESULTS FROM THE PUBMED SEARCH CONDUCTED ON 4 JULY 2021 AND 27 MAY 2022, USING THE '(AUTIS*[TITLE/ABSTRACT]) AND (COVID*[TITLE/ABSTRACT])' SEARCH FORMULA

PubMed ID	Article Title	Author(s)	Citation	Inclusion/Exclusion and Why
33367907[a]	Psychological and Behavioral Impact of Lockdown and Quarantine Measures for COVID-19 Pandemic on Children, Adolescents and Caregivers: A Systematic Review and Meta-Analysis	Panda PK, Gupta J, Chowdhury SR, Kumar R, Meena AK, Madaan P, Sharawat IK, Gulati S.	J Trop Pediatr. 2021 Jan 29; 67(1):fmaa122. doi: 10.1093/tropej/fmaa122.	Excluded – Study did not focus on the experiences of autistics and COVID-19 or their parents
33328021[a]	Psychiatric Disorders in Children and Adolescents during the COVID-19 Pandemic	Palacio-Ortiz JD, Londoño-Herrera JP, Nanclares-Márquez A, Robledo-Rengifo P, Quintero-Cadavid CP.	Rev Colomb Psiquiatr (Engl Ed). 2020 Oct-Dec;49(4): 279–288. doi: 10.1016/j.rcp.2020.05.006. Epub 2020 Jul 17.	Excluded – Study did not focus on the experiences of autistics and COVID-19 or their parents
33034366[a]	The Impact of COVID-19 on Children with Autism Spectrum Disorder	Amorim R, Catarino S, Miragaia P, Ferreras C, Viana V, Guardiano M.	Rev Neurol. 2020 Oct 16;71(8): 285–291. doi: 10.33588/rn.7108.2020381.	Excluded – Article published in Spanish
34112355[a]	Zinc	Skalny AV, Aschner M, Tinkov AA.	Adv Food Nutr Res. 2021;96: 251–310. doi: 10.1016/bs.afnr.2021.01.003. Epub 2021 May 24.	Excluded – Study did not focus on the experiences of autistics and COVID-19 or their parents
32416411[a]	COVID-19 and Autism	Steinman G.	Med Hypotheses. 2020 Sep; 142:109797. doi: 10.1016/j.mehy.2020.109797. Epub 2020 May 1.	Excluded – Study did not focus on the experiences of autistics and COVID-19 or their parents

32404232[a]	COVID-19 and People with Intellectual Disability: Impacts of a Pandemic	Courtenay K, Perera B.	Ir J Psychol Med. 2020 Sep; 37(3):231–236. doi: 10.1017/ipm.2020.45. Epub 2020 May 14.	Excluded – Study did not focus on the experiences of autistics and COVID-19 or their parents
33466265* [a]	Autism, Therapy and COVID-19	Sergi L, Mingione E, Ricci MC, Cavallaro A, Russo F, Corrivetti G, Operto FF, Frolli A.	Pediatr Rep. 2021 Jan 5;13(1): 35–44. doi: 10.3390/pediatric13010005.	Removed after the fourth step in PRISMA process
33921113[a]	COVID-19 and Pregnancy: Vertical Transmission and Inflammation Impact on Newborns	Joma M, Fovet CM, Seddiki N, Gressens P, Laforge M.	Vaccines (Basel). 2021 Apr 15; 9(4):391. doi: 10.3390/vaccines9040391.	Excluded – Study did not focus on the experiences of autistics and COVID-19 or their parents
33164601[a]	COVID-19 during Pregnancy and Postpartum	Naidu SAG, Clemens RA, Pressman P, Zaigham M, Kadkhoda K, Davies KJA, Naidu AS.	J Diet Suppl. 2022;19(1): 115–142. doi: 10.1080/19390211.2020.1834049. Epub 2020 Nov 8.	Excluded – Study did not focus on the experiences of autistics and COVID-19 or their parents
32986631[a]	The Impact of the COVID-19 Pandemic on Children with Autism Spectrum Disorders	Bellomo TR, Prasad S, Munzer T, Laventhal N.	J Pediatr Rehabil Med. 2020; 13(3):349–354. doi: 10.3233/PRM-200740.	Excluded – Opinion piece, commentary or letter to the editor
32998512[a]	Neurological, Neuropsychiatric and Neurodevelopmental Complications of COVID-19	Pantelis C, Jayaram M, Hannan AJ, Wesselingh R, Nithianantharajah J, Wannan CM, Syeda WT, Choy KC, Zantomio D, Christopoulos A, Velakoulis D, O'Brien TJ.	Aust N Z J Psychiatry. 2021 Aug;55(8):750–762. doi: 10.1177/0004867420961472. Epub 2020 Oct 1.	Excluded – Opinion piece, commentary or letter to the editor

(*Continued*)

PubMed ID	Article Title	Author(s)	Citation	Inclusion/Exclusion and Why
32998024[a]	Supporting Children with Neurodevelopmental Disorders during the COVID-19 Pandemic	Summers J, Baribeau D, Mockford M, Goldhopf L, Ambrozewicz P, Szatmari P, Vorstman J.	J Am Acad Child Adolesc Psychiatry. 2021 Jan;60(1): 2–6. doi: 10.1016/ j.jaac.2020.09.011. Epub 2020 Sep 27.	Excluded – Opinion piece, commentary or letter to the editor
33504101* [a]	A Qualitative Study of Child and Adolescent Mental Health during the COVID-19 Pandemic in Ireland	O'Sullivan K, Clark S, McGrane A, Rock N, Burke L, Boyle N, Joksimovic N, Marshall K.	Int J Environ Res Public Health. 2021 Jan 25;18(3): 1062. doi: 10.3390/ ijerph18031062.	Removed after the fourth step in PRISMA process
32503172[a]	Psychosocial and Behavioral Impact of COVID-19 in Autism Spectrum Disorder: An Online Parent Survey	Colizzi M, Sironi E, Antonini F, Ciceri ML, Bovo C, Zoccante L.	Brain Sci. 2020 Jun 3;10(6): 341. doi: 10.3390/ brainsci10060341.	Included in final analysis
33715904[a]	Vaccine Hesitancy and Anti-vaccination in the Time of COVID-19: A Google Trends Analysis	Pullan S, Dey M.	Vaccine. 2021 Apr 1;39(14): 1877–1881. doi: 10.1016/ j.vaccine.2021.03.019. Epub 2021 Mar 6.	Excluded – Study did not focus on the experiences of autistics and COVID-19 or their parents
34024500[a]	Maternal Nutrients and Effects of Gestational COVID-19 Infection on Fetal Brain Development	Hoffman MC, Freedman R, Law AJ, Clark AM, Hunter SK.	Clin Nutr ESPEN. 2021 Jun;43:1–8. doi: 10.1016/ j.clnesp.2021.04.019. Epub 2021 Apr 29.	Excluded – Study did not focus on the experiences of autistics and COVID-19 or their parents

33304279[a]	Behavioral Implications of the Covid-19 Process for Autism Spectrum Disorder, and Individuals' Comprehension of and Reactions to the Pandemic Conditions	Mutluer T, Doenyas C, Aslan Genc H.	Front Psychiatry. 2020 Nov 16; 11:561882. doi: 10.3389/fpsyt.2020.561882. eCollection 2020.	Included in final analysis
34002837[a]	Impact of COVID-19 Pandemic Lockdown on Occupational Therapy Practice and Use of Telerehabilitation – A Cross Sectional Study	Ganesan B, Fong KNK, Meena SK, Prasad P, Tong RKY.	Eur Rev Med Pharmacol Sci. 2021 May;25(9):3614–3622. doi: 10.26355/eurrev_202105_25845.	Excluded – Study did not focus on the experiences of autistics and COVID-19 or their parents
33229969[a]	Autism and Access to Care during the COVID-19 Crisis	Nadler C, Godwin DL, Dempsey J, Nyp SS.	J Dev Behav Pediatr. 2021 Jan 1;42(1):73–75. doi: 10.1097/DBP.0000000000000894.	Excluded – Case study
32445682[a]	COVID-19: Overcoming the Challenges Faced by Individuals with Autism and Their Families	Eshraghi AA, Li C, Alessandri M, Messinger DS, Eshraghi RS, Mittal R, Armstrong FD.	Lancet Psychiatry. 2020 Jun; 7(6):481–483. doi: 10.1016/S2215-0366(20)30197-8. Epub 2020 May 20.	Excluded – Opinion piece, commentary or letter to the editor
33649707[a]	COVID-19 Pandemic Effects in People with Autism Spectrum Disorder and Their Caregivers: Evaluation of Social Distancing and Lockdown Impact on Mental Health and General Status	Lugo-Marín J, Gisbert-Gustemps L, Setien-Ramos I, Español-Martín G, Ibañez-Jimenez P, Forner-Puntonet M, Arteaga-Henríquez G, Soriano-Día A, Duque-Yemail JD, Ramos-Quiroga JA.	Res Autism Spectr Disord. 2021 May;83:101757. doi: 10.1016/j.rasd.2021.101757. Epub 2021 Feb 25.	Included in final analysis

(Continued)

PubMed ID	Article Title	Author(s)	Citation	Inclusion/Exclusion and Why
33435701[a]	Core Experiences of Parents of Children with Autism during the COVID-19 Pandemic Lockdown	Tokatly Latzer I, Leitner Y, Karnieli-Miller O.	Autism. 2021 May;25(4): 1047–1059. doi: 10.1177/ 1362361320984317. Epub 2021 Jan 12.	Included in final analysis
33915884[a]	Quality of Life Changes during the COVID-19 Pandemic for Caregivers of Children with ADHD and/or ASD	Pecor KW, Barbayannis G, Yang M, Johnson J, Materasso S, Borda M, Garcia D, Garla V, Ming X.	Int J Environ Res Public Health. 2021 Apr 1;18(7):3667. doi: 10.3390/ijerph18073667.	Excluded – Study did not focus on the experiences of autistics and COVID-19 or their parents
32808424[a]	Examining the Impact of COVID-19 in Ethnically Diverse Families with Young Children with Intellectual and Developmental Disabilities	Neece C, McIntyre LL, Fenning R.	J Intellect Disabil Res. 2020 Oct;64(10):739–749. doi: 10.1111/jir.12769. Epub 2020 Aug 18.	Excluded – Study did not focus on the experiences of autistics and COVID-19 or their parents
33271447[a]	Stress and Emotional Wellbeing of Parents Due to Change in Routine for Children with Autism Spectrum Disorder (ASD) at Home during COVID-19 Pandemic in Saudi Arabia	Alhuzimi T.	Res Dev Disabil. 2021 Jan; 108:103822. doi: 10.1016/ j.ridd.2020.103822. Epub 2020 Nov 30.	Included in final analysis
34459536[b]	Editorial: Are Our Kids Getting a Fair Deal?	Merry S.	Child Adolesc Ment Health. 2021 Sep;26(3):193–194. doi: 10.1111/camh.12498.	Excluded – Opinion piece, commentary or letter to the editor

32932951[a]	Autism and COVID-19: A Case Series in a Neurodevelopmental Unit	Nollace L, Cravero C, Abbou A, Mazda-Walter B, Bleibtreu A, Pereirra N, Sainte-Marie M, Cohen D, Giannitelli M.	J Clin Med. 2020 Sep 11;9(9): 2937. doi: 10.3390/jcm9092937.	Excluded – Study did not focus on the experiences of autistics and COVID-19 or their parents
34619812[b]	Autism and COVID-19: Clinical Considerations	Naguy A, Pridmore S, Alamiri B.	Prim Care Companion CNS Disord. 2021 Oct 7;23(5): 21com03035. doi: 10.4088/PCC.21com03035.	Excluded – Opinion piece, commentary or letter to the editor
34393463[b]	Autistic Traits and Gender Modulate Emotion Changes before and during the COVID-19 Pandemic	Zhao X, Zhao B, Li W, Cai Y, Shi W, Li C.	Curr Psychol. 2021 Aug 7: 1–11. doi: 10.1007/s12144-021-02170-z. Online ahead of print.	Excluded – Study did not focus on the experiences of autistics and COVID-19 or their parents
35363281[b]	Autism and COVID-19	Fernandes P, Kwak H.	Pediatrics. 2022 Apr 1; 149(Suppl 4):e2020049437O. doi: 10.1542/peds.2020-049437O.	Excluded – Opinion piece, commentary or letter to the editor
34792882[b]	Neurological Complications of COVID-19: Review of Literature and Own Experience	Prikazchikov SV, Generalov VO, Sadykov TR, Mamedov LA.	Probl Sotsialnoi Gig Zdravookhranenniiai Istor Med. 2021 Aug;29(Special Issue):1304–1310. doi: 10.32687/0869-866X-2021-29-s2-1304-1310.	Excluded – Article published in Russian

(*Continued*)

PubMed ID	Article Title	Author(s)	Citation	Inclusion/Exclusion and Why
32474941[a]	Editorial Perspective: Perils and Promise for Child and Adolescent Sleep and Associated Psychopathology during the COVID-19 Pandemic	Becker SP, Gregory AM.	J Child Psychol Psychiatry. 2020 Jul;61(7):757–759. doi: 10.1111/jcpp.13278. Epub 2020 May 31.	Excluded – Opinion piece, commentary or letter to the editor
32779748[a]	Editorial Perspective: COVID-19 Pandemic-Related Psychopathology in Children and Adolescents with Mental Illness	Jefsen OH, Rohde C, Nørremark B, Østergaard SD.	J Child Psychol Psychiatry. 2021 Jun;62(6):798–800. doi: 10.1111/jcpp.13292. Epub 2020 Jul 7.	Excluded – Opinion piece, commentary or letter to the editor
34001500[a]	COVID-19 Health and Social Care Access for Autistic People: European Policy Review	Oakley B, Tillmann J, Ruigrok A, Baranger A, Takow C, Charman T, Jones E, Cusack J, Doherty M, Violland P, Wroczyńska A, Simonoff E, Buitelaar JK, Gallagher L, Murphy DGM; AIMS-2-TRIALS ECRAN & the AIMS-2-TRIALS Consortium.	BMJ Open. 2021 May 17; 11(6):e045341. doi: 10.1136/bmjopen-2020-045341.	Excluded – Opinion piece, commentary or letter to the editor
34203463[a]	A Pilot Study on Covid and Autism: Prevalence, Clinical Presentation and Vaccine Side Effects	Brondino N, Bertoglio F, Forneris F, Faravelli S, Borghesi A, Damiani S, Provenzani U, Nola M, Olivola M, Caviglia M, Politi P, Fusar-Poli L, Fusar-Poli P.	Brain Sci. 2021 Jun 28;11(7): 860. doi: 10.3390/brainsci11070860.	Excluded – Study did not focus on the experiences of autistics and COVID-19 or their parents

33736746[a]	COVID-19-Related Prescribing Challenge in Intellectual Disability	Rauf B, Sheikh H, Majid H, Roy A, Pathania R.	BJPsych Open. 2021 Mar 19; 7(2):e66. doi: 10.1192/bjo.2021.26.	Excluded – Study did not focus on the experiences of autistics and COVID-19 or their parents
34611574[b]	COVID-19 and Food-Related Outcomes in Children with Autism Spectrum Disorder: Disparities by Income and Food Security Status	Panjwani AA, Bailey RL, Kelleher BL.	Curr Dev Nutr. 2021 Sep 3; 5(9):nzab112. doi: 10.1093/cdn/nzab112. eCollection 2021 Sep.	Included in the post-survey analysis
34173571[a]	COVID-19 and Autism: Uncertainty, Distress and Feeling Forgotten	Patel JA, Badiani AA, Nielsen FBH, Assi S, Unadkat V, Patel B, Courtney C, Hallas L.	Public Health Pract (Oxf). 2020 Nov;1:100034. doi: 10.1016/j.puhip.2020.100034. Epub 2020 Dec 22.	Excluded – Opinion piece, commentary or letter to the editor
33913261[a]	The Impact of COVID-19 on Stress, Anxiety, and Coping in Youth with and Without Autism and Their Parents	Corbett BA, Muscatello RA, Klemencic ME, Schwartzman JM.	Autism Res. 2021 Jul;14(7): 1496–1511. doi: 10.1002/aur.2521. Epub 2021 Apr 29.	Included in final analysis
33679571[a]	Neurologic Care of COVID-19 in Children	Boronat S.	Front Neurol. 2021 Feb 18;11: 613832. doi: 10.3389/fneur.2020.613832. eCollection 2020.	Excluded – Study did not focus on the experiences of autistics and COVID-19 or their parents
32405083[a]	Appreciating COVID-19 as a Child and Adolescent Psychiatrist on the Move	Cohen D.	Encephale. 2020 Jun;46(3S): S99-S106. doi: 10.1016/j.encep.2020.05.005. Epub 2020 May 13.	Excluded – Article published in French

(*Continued*)

PubMed ID	Article Title	Author(s)	Citation	Inclusion/Exclusion and Why
33434768[a]	Social Communication of Affective States	Sterley TL, Bains JS.	Curr Opin Neurobiol. 2021 Jun;68:44–51. doi: 10.1016/j.conb.2020.12.007. Epub 2021 Jan 9.	Excluded – Study did not focus on the experiences of autistics and COVID-19 or their parents
35321368[b]	Psycho-Social Consequences Associated with COVID-19 in People with ASD and Their Families: A Literature Review	Aarabi MA, Abdi K, Khanjani MS.	Med J Islam Repub Iran. 2021 Oct 7;35:131. doi: 10.47176/mjiri.35.131. eCollection 2021.	Included in the post-survey analysis
33984425[a]	Editorial: Mental Health and Schools: Has the Time Arrived?	Pumariega AJ.	J Am Acad Child Adolesc Psychiatry. 2021 Dec;60(12):1454–1456. doi: 10.1016/j.jaac.2021.05.001. Epub 2021 May 11.	Excluded – Study did not focus on the experiences of autistics and COVID-19 or their parents
34508208[b]	The New Normal – Dentistry and the Autistic Patient	Bellis W.	Br Dent J. 2021 Sep;231(5):303–304. doi: 10.1038/s41415-021-3376-2. Epub 2021 Sep 10.	Excluded – Opinion piece, commentary or letter to the editor
34147945* [a]	COVID-19 and Behaviors in Children with Autism Spectrum Disorder: Disparities by Income and Food Security Status	Panjwani AA, Bailey RL, Kelleher BL.	Res Dev Disabil. 2021 Aug;115:104002. doi: 10.1016/j.ridd.2021.104002. Epub 2021 Jun 1.	Removed after the fourth step in PRISMA process

33735741[a]	COVID-19 and Social Responsiveness: A Comparison between Children with Sotos Syndrome and Autism	Siracusano M, Riccioni A, Fagiolo I, Segatori E, Gialloreti LE, Galasso C, Curatolo P, Mazzone L.	Psychiatry Res. 2021 May; 299:113851. doi: 10.1016/ j.psychres.2021.113851. Epub 2021 Mar 2.	Excluded – Study did not focus on the experiences of autistics and COVID-19 or their parents
34114135[a]	Telehealth and Autism Prior to and in the Age of COVID-19: A Systematic and Critical Review of the Last Decade	Ellison KS, Guidry J, Picou P, Adenuga P, Davis TE 3rd.	Clin Child Fam Psychol Rev. 2021 Sep;24(3):599–630. doi: 10.1007/s10567-021-00358-0. Epub 2021 Jun 10.	Excluded – Opinion piece, commentary or letter to the editor
34351096[b]	Autism Screening Tests: A Narrative Review	Fekar Gharamaleki F, Bahrami B, Masumi J.	J Public Health Res. 2021 Aug 5;11(1):2308. doi: 10.4081/ jphr.2021.2308.	Excluded – Study did not focus on the experiences of autistics and COVID-19 or their parents
33206719[a]	Clinical and Molecular Characterization of COVID-19 Hospitalized Patients	Benetti E, Giliberti A, Emiliozzi A, Valentino F, Bergantini L, Fallerini C, Anedda F, Amitrano S, Conticini E, Tita R, d'Alessandro M, Fava F, Marcantonio S, Baldassarri M, Bruttini M, Mazzei MA, Montagnani F, Mandalà M, Bargagli E, Furini S; GEN-COVID Multicenter Study, Renieri A, Mari F.	PLoS One. 2020 Nov 18; 15(11):e0242534. doi: 10.1371/ journal.pone.0242534. eCollection 2020.	Excluded – Study did not focus on the experiences of autistics and COVID-19 or their parents

(*Continued*)

PubMed ID	Article Title	Author(s)	Citation	Inclusion/Exclusion and Why
33559334[a]	Early Pandemic Experiences of Autistic Adults: Predictors of Psychological Distress	Bal VH, Wilkinson E, White LC, Law JK; SPARK Consortium, Feliciano P, Chung WK.	Autism Res. 2021 Jun;14(6): 1209–1219. doi: 10.1002/aur.2480. Epub 2021 Feb 8.	Included in the final analysis
34580666[b]	Mental Health and Social Support of Caregivers of Children and Adolescents with ASD and Other Developmental Disorders during COVID-19 Pandemic	Wang C.	J Affect Disord Rep. 2021 Dec; 6:100242. doi: 10.1016/j.jadr.2021.100242. Epub 2021 Sep 22.	Included in the post-survey analysis
34591588[b]	School-Based Autism Evaluations in the COVID-19 Era	Brunson McClain M, Roanhorse TT, Harris B, Heyborne M, Zemantic PK, Azad G.	Sch Psychol. 2021 Sep;36(5): 377–387. doi: 10.1037/spq0000447.	Excluded – Study did not focus on the experiences of autistics and COVID-19 or their parents
33802042* [a]	Association between Viral Infections and Risk of Autistic Disorder: An Overview	Shuid AN, Jayusman PA, Shuid N, Ismail J, Kamal Nor N, Mohamed IN.	Int J Environ Res Public Health. 2021 Mar 10;18(6): 2817. doi: 10.3390/ijerph18062817.	Removed after the fourth step in PRISMA process
34545706[b]	The Association between COVID-19, Personal Wellbeing, Depression, and Suicide risk Factors in Australian Autistic Adults	Hedley D, Hayward SM, Denney K, Uljarević M, Bury S, Sahin E, Brown CM, Clapperton A, Dissanayake C, Robinson J, Trollor J, Stokes MA.	Autism Res. 2021 Dec;14(12): 2663–2676. doi: 10.1002/aur.2614. Epub 2021 Sep 21.	Included in the post-survey analysis

33758930[a]	Families with Children with Neurodevelopmental Disorders during COVID-19: A Scoping Review	Shorey S, Lau LST, Tan JX, Ng ED, Aishworiya R.	J Pediatr Psychol. 2021 Jun 3; 46(5):514–525. doi: 10.1093/jpepsy/jsab029.	Excluded – Study did not focus on the experiences of autistics and COVID-19 or their parents
34293632[b]	Differences in Emotional State and Autistic Symptoms before and during Confinement Due to the COVID-19 Pandemic	Martínez-González AE, Moreno-Amador B, Piqueras JA.	Res Dev Disabil. 2021 Sep; 116:104038. doi: 10.1016/j.ridd.2021.104038. Epub 2021 Jul 16.	Included in the post-survey analysis
33998265[a]	Preventing the Next Pandemic and Tackling Antiscience: An Interview with Peter Hotez	Hotez P.	Future Microbiol. 2021 May; 16:539–541. doi: 10.2217/fmb-2021-0088. Epub 2021 May 17.	Excluded – Study did not focus on the experiences of autistics and COVID-19 or their parents
34591373[b]	The Impact of COVID-19 on the Mental Health and Wellbeing of Caregivers of Autistic Children and Youth: A Scoping Review	Lee V, Albaum C, Tablon Modica P, Ahmad F, Gorter JW, Khanlou N, McMorris C, Lai J, Harrison C, Hedley T, Johnston P, Putterman C, Spoelstra M, Weiss JA.	Autism Res. 2021 Dec;14(12): 2477–2494. doi: 10.1002/aur.2616. Epub 2021 Sep 30.	Included in the post-survey analysis
34077795[b]	The Progress of Chemokines and Chemokine Receptors in Autism Spectrum Disorders	Ye J, Wang H, Cui L, Chu S, Chen N.	Brain Res Bull. 2021 Sep;174: 268–280. doi: 10.1016/j.brainresbull.2021.05.024. Epub 2021 May 30.	Excluded – Study did not focus on the experiences of autistics and COVID-19 or their parents

(Continued)

PubMed ID	Article Title	Author(s)	Citation	Inclusion/Exclusion and Why
32698850[a]	Coping, Fostering Resilience, and Driving Care Innovation for Autistic People and Their Families during the COVID-19 Pandemic and Beyond	Ameis SH, Lai MC, Mulsant BH, Szatmari P.	Mol Autism. 2020 Jul 22;11(1): 61. doi: 10.1186/s13229-020-00365-y.	Excluded – Opinion piece, commentary or letter to the editor
34439660[b]	Parental Stress and Disability in Offspring: A Snapshot during the COVID-19 Pandemic	Siracusano M, Riccioni A, Gialloreti LE, Segatori E, Arturi L, Vasta M, Porfirio MC, Terribili M, Galasso C, Mazzone L.	Brain Sci. 2021 Aug 5;11(8): 1040. doi: 10.3390/brainsci11081040.	Excluded – Study did not focus on the experiences of autistics and COVID-19 or their parents
33831811[a]	Autistic Traits and Negative Emotions in the General Population during COVID-19: Mediating Roles of the Behavioural Immune System and COVID-19 Risk Perception	Zhao X, Shi W, Li X, Li W, Li C.	Psychiatry Res. 2021 Jun;300: 113918. doi: 10.1016/j.psychres.2021.113918. Epub 2021 Apr 1.	Excluded – Study did not focus on the experiences of autistics and COVID-19 or their parents
33901700[a]	Psychological Impact during COVID-19 Lockdown in Children and Adolescents with Previous Mental Health Disorders	Lopez-Serrano J, Díaz-Bóveda R, González-Vallespí L, Santamarina-Pérez P, Bretones-Rodríguez A, Calvo R, Lera-Miguel S.	Rev Psiquiatr Salud Ment (Engl Ed). 2021 Apr 24: S1888-9891(21)00035-5. doi: 10.1016/j.rpsm.2021.04.002. Online ahead of print.	Excluded – Study did not focus on the experiences of autistics and COVID-19 or their parents

34553489[b]	Rethinking Autism Spectrum Disorder Assessment for Children during COVID-19 and Beyond	Zwaigenbaum L, Bishop S, Stone WL, Ibanez L, Halladay A, Goldman S, Kelly A, Klaiman C, Lai MC, Miller M, Saulnier C, Siper P, Sohl K, Warren Z, Wetherby A.	Autism Res. 2021 Nov;14(11): 2251–2259. doi: 10.1002/ aur.2615. Epub 2021 Sep 22.	Excluded – Study did not focus on the experiences of autistics and COVID-19 or their parents
33662654[a]	Impact of Containment and Mitigation Measures on Children and Youth with ASD during the COVID-19 pandemic: Report from the ELENA Cohort	Berard M, Rattaz C, Peries M, Loubersac J, Munir K, Baghdadli A.	J Psychiatr Res. 2021 May; 137:73–80. doi: 10.1016/ j.jpsychires.2021.02.041. Epub 2021 Feb 22.	Included in final analysis
34423522[b]	The Relationship between Irritability and autism Symptoms in Children with ASD in COVID-19 Home Confinement Period	Türkoğlu S, Uçar HN, Çetin FH, Güler HA, Tezcan ME.	Int J Clin Pract. 2021 Nov; 75(11):e14742. doi: 10.1111/ ijcp.14742. Epub 2021 Aug 30.	Included in the post-survey analysis
34369382[b]	Digital Mental Health and Neurodevelopmental Services: Case-Based Realist Evaluation	Burbach FR, Stiles KM.	JMIR Form Res. 2021 Sep 17; 5(9):e29845. doi: 10.2196/ 29845.	Excluded – Study did not focus on the experiences of autistics and COVID-19 or their parents
32592337[a]	COVID-19 and Autism Research: Perspectives from Around the Globe	Amaral DG, de Vries PJ.	Autism Res. 2020 Jun;13(6): 844–869. doi: 10.1002/ aur.2329.	Excluded – Study did not focus on the experiences of autistics and COVID-19 or their parents

(*Continued*)

PubMed ID	Article Title	Author(s)	Citation	Inclusion/Exclusion and Why
33856853[a]	Comparing the Initial Impact of COVID-19 on Burden and Psychological Distress among Family Caregivers of Children with and Without Developmental Disabilities	Chafouleas SM, Iovino EA.	Sch Psychol. 2021 Sep;36(5): 358–366. doi: 10.1037/spq0000426. Epub 2021 Apr 15.	Excluded – Study did not focus on the experiences of autistics and COVID-19 or their parents
33841149[a]	Head-to-Head Comparison of Sedation and Somnolence among 37 Antipsychotics in Schizophrenia, Bipolar Disorder, Major Depression, Autism Spectrum Disorders, Delirium, and Repurposed in COVID-19, Infectious Diseases, and Oncology from the FAERS, 2004–2020	Eugene AR, Eugene B, Masiak M, Masiak JS.	Front Pharmacol. 2021 Mar 25;12:621691. doi: 10.3389/fphar.2021.621691. eCollection 2021.	Excluded – Study did not focus on the experiences of autistics and COVID-19 or their parents
34573161[b]	Changes in Sleep Patterns and Disorders in Children and Adolescents with Attention Deficit Hyperactivity Disorders and Autism Spectrum Disorders during the COVID-19 Lockdown	Bruni O, Breda M, Ferri R, Melegari MG.	Brain Sci. 2021 Aug 27;11(9): 1139. doi: 10.3390/brainsci11091139.	Excluded – Study did not focus on the experiences of autistics and COVID-19 or their parents
34720549[b]	Investigating the Effects of COVID-19 Lockdown on Italian Children and Adolescents with and Without Neurodevelopmental Disorders: A Cross-Sectional Study	Termine C, Dui LG, Borzaga L, Galli V, Lipari R, Vergani M, Berlusconi V, Agosti M, Lunardini F, Ferrante S.	Curr Psychol. 2021 Oct 25: 1–17. doi: 10.1007/s12144-021-02321-2. Online ahead of print.	Excluded – Study did not focus on the experiences of autistics and COVID-19 or their parents

34262075[b]	Social Cognition in Individuals Born Preterm	Pavlova MA, Galli J, Zanetti F, Pagani F, Micheletti S, Rossi A, Sokolov AN, Fallgatter AJ, Fazzi EM.	Sci Rep. 2021 Jul 14;11(1): 14448. doi: 10.1038/s41598-021-93709-4.	Excluded – Study did not focus on the experiences of autistics and COVID-19 or their parents
32928535[a]	Immunopsychiatry and SARS-CoV-2 Pandemic: Links and Possible Consequences	Daaboul J, Tamouza R, Leboyer M.	Encephale. 2021 Apr;47(2): 151–156. doi: 10.1016/j.encep.2020.07.002. Epub 2020 Jul 21.	Excluded – Article published in French
33772777* [a]	Tolerance of Face Coverings for Children with Autism Spectrum Disorder	Halbur M, Kodak T, McKee M, Carroll R, Preas E, Reidy J, Cordeiro MC.	J Appl Behav Anal. 2021 Apr; 54(2):600–617. doi: 10.1002/jaba.833. Epub 2021 Mar 26.	Removed after the fourth step in PRISMA process
34448995[b]	Predictors of Satisfaction with Autism Treatment Services during COVID-19	Ferguson EF, Jimenez-Muñoz M, Feerst H, Vernon TW.	J Autism Dev Disord. 2021 Aug 27:1–12. doi: 10.1007/s10803-021-05232-0. Online ahead of print.	Excluded – Study did not focus on the experiences of autistics and COVID-19 or their parents
34231323[b]	Psychiatric Problems during the COVID-19 Pandemic in Children with Autism Spectrum Disorder	Vasa RA, Singh V, Holingue C, Kalb LG, Jang Y, Keefer A.	Autism Res. 2021 Oct;14(10): 2113–2119. doi: 10.1002/aur.2574. Epub 2021 Jul 7.	Included in the post-survey analysis
34240291[b]	Mental Health and Resilient Coping in Caregivers of Autistic Individuals during the COVID-19 Pandemic: Findings from the Families Facing COVID Study	Friesen KA, Weiss JA, Howe SJ, Kerns CM, McMorris CA.	J Autism Dev Disord. 2021 Jul 8:1–11. doi: 10.1007/s10803-021-05177-4. Online ahead of print.	Included in the post-survey analysis

(*Continued*)

PubMed ID	Article Title	Author(s)	Citation	Inclusion/Exclusion and Why
33101602[a]	ABA Finding Its Heart during a Pandemic: An Exploration in Social Validity	Nicolson AC, Lazo-Pearson JF, Shandy J.	Behav Anal Pract. 2020 Oct 16;13(4):757–766. doi: 10.1007/s40617-020-00517-9. eCollection 2020 Dec.	Excluded – Opinion piece, commentary or letter to the editor
33418151[a]	Isolating Residents Including Wandering Residents in Care and Group Homes: Medical Ethics and English Law in the Context of Covid-19	Liddell K, Ruck Keene A, Holland A, Huppert J, Underwood BR, Clark O, Barclay SIG.	Int J Law Psychiatry. 2021 Jan-Feb;74:101649. doi: 10.1016/ j.ijlp.2020.101649. Epub 2020 Dec 1.	Excluded – Study did not focus on the experiences of autistics and COVID-19 or their parents
33753983[a]	COVID-19: Practice and Ethics of Videoconsultation Assessment of Children with Autism Spectrum Disorder	Doyen C, Kaye K.	Ethique Sante. 2021 Jun;18(2): 74–80. doi: 10.1016/ j.etiqe.2021.03.001. Epub 2021 Mar 18.	Excluded – Article published in French
34725409[b]	An mCARE Study on Patterns of risk and Resilience for Children with ASD in Bangladesh	Rabbani M, Haque MM, Das Dipal D, Zarif MII, Iqbal A, Schwichtenberg A, Bansal N, Soron TR, Ahmed SI, Ahamed SI.	Sci Rep. 2021 Nov 1;11(1): 21342. doi: 10.1038/s41598-021-00793-7.	Excluded – Study did not focus on the experiences of autistics and COVID-19 or their parents
32328220[a]	A Proposed Process for Risk Mitigation during the COVID-19 Pandemic	Cox DJ, Plavnick JB, Brodhead MT.	Behav Anal Pract. 2020 Apr 23;13(2):299–305. doi: 10.1007/s40617-020-00430-1. eCollection 2020 Jun.	Excluded – Opinion piece, commentary or letter to the editor

33692639[a]	Impact of the COVID-19 Pandemic on Children with ASD and Their Families: An Online Survey in China	Huang S, Sun T, Zhu Y, Song S, Zhang J, Huang L, Chen Q, Peng G, Zhao D, Yu H, Jing J.	Psychol Res Behav Manag. 2021 Mar 4;14:289–297. doi: 10.2147/PRBM.S293426. eCollection 2021.	Included in final analysis
33845620[a]	Ten Weeks in: COVID-19-Related Distress in Adults with Autism Spectrum Disorder	Adams RE, Zheng S, Taylor JL, Bishop SL.	Autism. 2021 Oct;25(7): 2140–2145. doi: 10.1177/13623613211005919. Epub 2021 Apr 12.	Included in final analysis
33913138[a]	Impact of COVID-19 on Patients from FACT or Autism Teams	Castelein S, Bruins J, van Balkom IDC.	Tijdschr Psychiatr. 2021;63(4): 250–256.	Excluded – Article published in Dutch
32505067[a]	Could Autism Spectrum Disorders be a Risk Factor for COVID-19?	Lima MES, Barros LCM, Aragão GF.	Med Hypotheses. 2020 Nov; 144:109899. doi: 10.1016/j.mehy.2020.109899. Epub 2020 May 30.	Excluded – Opinion piece, commentary or letter to the editor
33829918[a]	Availability of Services and Caregiver Burden: Supporting Individuals with Neurogenetic Conditions during the COVID-19 Pandemic	Kowanda M, Cartner L, Kentros C, Geltzeiler AR, Singer KE, Weaver WC, Lehman CD, Smith S, Smith RS, Walsh LK, Diehl K, Nagpal N, Brooks E, Mebane CM, Wilson AL, Marvin AR, White LC, Law JK, Jensen W, Daniels AM, Tjernagel J, Snyder LG, Taylor CM, Chung WK.	J Child Neurol. 2021 Aug; 36(9):760–767. doi: 10.1177/08830738211001209. Epub 2021 Apr 8.	Excluded – Study did not focus on the experiences of autistics and COVID-19 or their parents

(Continued)

PubMed ID	Article Title	Author(s)	Citation	Inclusion/Exclusion and Why
32637293[a]	An Essential Service Decision Model for ABA Providers during Crisis	Colombo RA, Wallace M, Taylor R.	Behav Anal Pract. 2020 May 22;13(2):306–311. doi: 10.1007/s40617-020-00432-z. eCollection 2020 Jun.	Excluded – Opinion piece, commentary or letter to the editor
34473008[b]	Telehealth Diagnosis of Autism Spectrum Disorder Through Clinical Cases	Ludwig NN, Child AE, Jashar DT, Mostow AJ, Wodka EL.	Clin Neuropsychol. 2021 Sep 2:1–21. doi: 10.1080/13854046.2021.1970228. Online ahead of print.	Excluded – Study did not focus on the experiences of autistics and COVID-19 or their parents
33632259[a]	The relationship between 2019-nCoV and Psychological Distress among Parents of children with Autism Spectrum Disorder	Wang L, Li D, Pan S, Zhai J, Xia W, Sun C, Zou M.	Global Health. 2021 Feb 25; 17(1):23. doi: 10.1186/s12992-021-00674-8.	Included in final analysis
32899799[a]	Prevalence and Associated Factors of Emotional and Behavioural Difficulties during COVID-19 Pandemic in Children with Neurodevelopmental Disorders	Nonweiler J, Rattray F, Baulcomb J, Happé F, Absoud M.	Children (Basel). 2020 Sep 4; 7(9):128. doi: 10.3390/children7090128.	Excluded – Study did not focus on the experiences of autistics and COVID-19 or their parents

34539246[b]	Educators' Experiences in Special Education Institutions during the COVID-19 Outbreak	Yakut AD.	J Res Spec Educ Needs. 2021 Jul 15:10.1111/1471-3802.12533. doi: 10.1111/1471-3802.12533. Online ahead of print.	Excluded – Study did not focus on the experiences of autistics and COVID-19 or their parents
34621194[b]	The Impact of COVID-19 on Sleep in Autistic Adults: Longitudinal Comparisons pre and during Lockdown	Halstead EJ, Sullivan EC, Dimitriou D.	Front Psychiatry. 2021 Sep 21; 12:708339. doi: 10.3389/fpsyt.2021.708339. eCollection 2021.	Included in the post-survey analysis
34169750[a]	'Anything but the Phone!': Communication Mode Preferences in the Autism Community	Howard PL, Sedgewick F.	Autism. 2021 Nov;25(8): 2265–2278. doi: 10.1177/13623613211014995. Epub 2021 Jun 25.	Excluded – Study did not focus on the experiences of autistics and COVID-19 or their parents
35136254[b]	Coping with Autism during Lockdown Period of the COVID-19 Pandemic: A Cross-Sectional Survey	Kaku SM, Chandran S, Roopa N, Choudhary A, Ramesh J, Somashekariah S, Kuduvalli S, Rao VS, Mysore A.	Indian J Psychiatry. 2021 Nov-Dec;63(6):568–574. doi: 10.4103/indianjpsychiatry.indianjpsychiatry_344_21. Epub 2021 Dec 3.	Included in the post-survey analysis
33836625[a]	Short Report on Research Trends during the COVID-19 Pandemic and use of Telehealth Interventions and Remote Brain Research in Children with Autism Spectrum Disorder	Su WC, Srinivasan S, Cleffi C, Bhat A.	Autism. 2021 Aug;25(6): 1816–1822. doi: 10.1177/13623613211004795. Epub 2021 Apr 9.	Excluded – Opinion piece, commentary or letter to the editor

(*Continued*)

PubMed ID	Article Title	Author(s)	Citation	Inclusion/Exclusion and Why
34581522[b]	Why Fast COVID-19 Vaccination Needed for People with Disabilities and Autistics in Korea?	Yoon WH.	J Korean Med Sci. 2021 Sep 27;36(37):e267. doi: 10.3346/jkms.2021.36.e267.	Excluded – Opinion piece, commentary or letter to the editor
33118913[a]	Priority Concerns for People with Intellectual and Developmental Disabilities during the COVID-19 Pandemic	Tromans S, Kinney M, Chester V, Alexander R, Roy A, Sander JW, Dudson H, Shankar R.	BJPsych Open. 2020 Oct 29; 6(6):e128. doi: 10.1192/bjo.2020.122.	Excluded – Study did not focus on the experiences of autistics and COVID-19 or their parents
33977886[a]	Effects of the COVID-19 Pandemic on Mental Healthcare and Services: Results of a UK Survey of Front-Line Staff Working with People with Intellectual disability and/or Autism	Sheehan R, Dalton-Locke C, Ali A, Vera San Juan N, Totsika V, Hassiotis A.	BJPsych Bull. 2021 May 12: 1–7. doi: 10.1192/bjb.2021.52. Online ahead of print.	Excluded – Study did not focus on the experiences of autistics and COVID-19 or their parents
33521688[a]	COVID-19 Impacts the Expression of Molecular Markers Associated with Neuropsychiatric Disorders	Quincozes-Santos A, Rosa RL, Tureta EF, Bobermin LD, Berger M, Guimarães JA, Santi L, Beys-da-Silva WO.	Brain Behav Immun Health. 2021 Feb;11:100196. doi: 10.1016/j.bbih.2020.100196. Epub 2020 Dec 28.	Excluded – Study did not focus on the experiences of autistics and COVID-19 or their parents
34196450[a]	A Quantitative Evaluation of a Regional Positive Behavioural Support Workforce Development Approach	McKenzie K, Murray G, Martin R, Murray A, Metcalfe D.	J Appl Res Intellect Disabil. 2021 Nov;34(6):1641–1654. doi: 10.1111/jar.12915. Epub 2021 Jul 1.	Excluded – Study did not focus on the experiences of autistics and COVID-19 or their parents

34261711[b]	Caregiver Burnout, Gaps in Care, and COVID-19: Effects on Families of Youth with Autism and Intellectual Disability	Young E, Milligan K, Henze M, Johnson S, Weyman K.	Can Fam Physician. 2021 Jul; 67(7):506–508. doi: 10.46747/cfp.6707506.	Excluded – Study did not focus on the experiences of autistics and COVID-19 or their parents
34178884[a]	Risks and Protective Factors Associated with Mental Health Symptoms during COVID-19 Home Confinement in Italian Children and Adolescents: The #Understandingkids Study	Oliva S, Russo G, Gili R, Russo L, Di Mauro A, Spagnoli A, Alunni Fegatelli D, Romani M, Costa A, Veraldi S, Manti F.	Front Pediatr. 2021 Jun 11;9: 664702. doi: 10.3389/fped.2021.664702. eCollection 2021.	Excluded – Study did not focus on the experiences of autistics and COVID-19 or their parents
32837705[a]	Creating and Sharing Digital ABA Instructional Activities: A Practical Tutorial	Mattson SL, Higbee TS, Aguilar J, Nichols B, Campbell VE, Nix LD, Reinert KS, Peck S, Lewis K.	Behav Anal Pract. 2020 Jul 23; 13(4):1–27. doi: 10.1007/s40617-020-00440-z. Online ahead of print.	Excluded – Study did not focus on the experiences of autistics and COVID-19 or their parents
32712636[a]	Autism Spectrum Disorder and COVID-19: Helping Caregivers Navigate the Pandemic	Lim T, Tan MY, Aishworiya R, Kang YQ.	Ann Acad Med Singap. 2020 Jun;49(6):384–386.	Excluded – Opinion piece, commentary or letter to the editor
33486423[a]	The Pediatric Neurology 2020 Research Workforce Survey: Optimism in a Time of Challenge	Bonkowsky JL, Felling RJ, Grinspan ZM, Guerriero RM, Kosofsky BE, Lyons-Warren AM, deVeber GA.	Pediatr Neurol. 2021 Mar;116: 62–67. doi: 10.1016/j.pediatrneurol.2020.11.020. Epub 2020 Dec 3.	Excluded – Study did not focus on the experiences of autistics and COVID-19 or their parents

(*Continued*)

PubMed ID	Article Title	Author(s)	Citation	Inclusion/Exclusion and Why
34456303[b]	The Value of Telehealth and a Team-Based Approach in Improving Developmental and Behavioral Care during the COVID-19 Pandemic	Barnhardt EW, Steingass K, Levine A, Jurbank M, Piercefield J, Nyp SS.	J Dev Behav Pediatr. 2021 Sep 1;42(7):602–604. doi: 10.1097/ DBP.0000000000000997.	Excluded – Study did not focus on the experiences of autistics and COVID-19 or their parents
33964709[a]	Psychological Distress and Burden among Family Caregivers of Children with and Without Developmental Disabilities Six Months into the COVID-19 Pandemic	Iovino EA, Caemmerer J, Chafouleas SM.	Res Dev Disabil. 2021 Jul;114: 103983. doi: 10.1016/ j.ridd.2021.103983. Epub 2021 May 5.	Excluded – Study did not focus on the experiences of autistics and COVID-19 or their parents
34811386[b]	The (a)typical burden of COVID-19 pandemic scenario in Autism Spectrum Disorder	Fumagalli L, Nicoli M, Villa L, Riva V, Vicovaro M, Casartelli L.	Sci Rep. 2021 Nov 22;11(1): 22655. doi: 10.1038/s41598-021-01907-x.	Excluded – Study did not focus on the experiences of autistics and COVID-19 or their parents
33658046[a]	The Psychological Impact of the COVID-19 Pandemic on Adults with Autism: A Survey Study Across Three Countries	Oomen D, Nijhof AD, Wiersema JR.	Mol Autism. 2021 Mar 3;12(1): 21. doi: 10.1186/s13229-021-00424-y.	Included in final analysis

33326409[a]	Implementation of Telehealth Services to Assess, Monitor, and Treat Neurodevelopmental Disorders: Systematic Review	Valentine AZ, Hall SS, Young E, Brown BJ, Groom MJ, Hollis C, Hall CL.	J Med Internet Res. 2021 Jan 20;23(1):e22619. doi: 10.2196/22619.	Excluded – Study did not focus on the experiences of autistics and COVID-19 or their parents
34092836[a]	Experiences of Families of Autistic Children during a Period of Lockdown: Exploratory Study	Chamak B.	Neuropsychiatr Enfance Adolesc. 2021 Sep;69(5): 235–240. doi: 10.1016/j.neurenf.2021.05.003. Epub 2021 Jun 2.	Excluded – Article published in French
34659652[b]	Adapting Direct Services for Telehealth: A Practical Tutorial	Bergmann S, Toussaint KA, Niland H, Sansing EM, Armshaw G, Baltazar M.	Behav Anal Pract. 2021 Oct 12;14(4):1–37. doi: 10.1007/s40617-020-00529-5. Online ahead of print.	Excluded – Study did not focus on the experiences of autistics and COVID-19 or their parents
34988366[b]	Study Protocol for Autism Specific Transition Resources (T-Res Study): Developing a Flexible Resource Package for Dealing with the Loosening and/or Lifting of COVID-19 Related Restrictions	Smyth S, Mc Laughlin N, Egan C, Gurrin C, Quinn K, McGarrell M, Devlin S.	HRB Open Res. 2021 Jan 28; 4:12. doi: 10.12688/hrbopenres.13155.1. eCollection 2021.	Excluded – Study did not focus on the experiences of autistics and COVID-19 or their parents
33562872[a]	Medical Students and SARS-CoV-2 Vaccination: Attitude and Behaviors	Szmyd B, Bartoszek A, Karuga FF, Staniecka K, Błaszczyk M, Radek M.	Vaccines (Basel). 2021 Feb 5; 9(2):128. doi: 10.3390/vaccines9020128.	Excluded – Did not focus on the experiences of autistics and CODI-19 or their parents

(Continued)

PubMed ID	Article Title	Author(s)	Citation	Inclusion/Exclusion and Why
34306962[b]	Using Telehealth to Provide Interventions for Children with ASD: A Systematic Review	de Nocker YL, Toolan CK.	Rev J Autism Dev Disord. 2021 Jul 16:1–31. doi: 10.1007/s40489-021-00278-3. Online ahead of print.	Excluded – Did not focus on the experiences of autistics and CODI-19 or their parents
34350304[b]	How Providers in Child Neurology Transitioned to Telehealth during COVID-19 Pandemic	Bain JM, Dyer CA, Galvin M, Goldman S, Selman J, Silver WG, Tom SE.	Child Neurol Open. 2021 Jul 19;8:2329048X211022976. doi: 10.1177/2329048X211022976. eCollection 2021 Jan-Dec.	Excluded – Did not focus on the experiences of autistics and CODI-19 or their parents
34448994[b]	Experience of Autistic Children and Their Families during the Pandemic: From Distress to Coping Strategies	Jacques C, Saulnier G, Éthier A, Soulières I.	J Autism Dev Disord. 2021 Aug 27:1–13. doi: 10.1007/s10803-021-05233-z. Online ahead of print.	Included in the post-survey analysis
34624722[b]	The Impact of COVID-19 Pandemic Social Restrictions on Individuals with Autism Spectrum Disorder and Their Caregivers in the Stateof Qatar: A Cross-Sectional Study	Khan YS, Khan AW, Tahir ME, Hammoudeh S, Shamlawi MA, Alabdulla M.	Res Dev Disabil. 2021 Dec;119:104090. doi: 10.1016/j.ridd.2021.104090. Epub 2021 Sep 30.	Included in the post-survey analysis
33759380[a]	A lost Generation? The Impact of the COVID-19 Pandemic on Early Career ASD Researchers	Harrop C, Bal V, Carpenter K, Halladay A.	Autism Res. 2021 Jun;14(6):1078–1087. doi: 10.1002/aur.2503. Epub 2021 Mar 24.	Excluded – Opinion piece, commentary or letter to the editor

34897755[b]	Fear, Changes in Routine and Dental Care for Children and Adolescents with Autism Spectrum Disorder in the COVID-19 Pandemic: A Survey with Brazilian Parents	Azevedo Machado B, Silva Moro J, Massignam C, Cardoso M, Bolan M.	Spec Care Dentist. 2021 Dec 13. doi: 10.1111/scd.12683. Online ahead of print.	Included in the post-survey analysis
33090358[a]	Perceptions of Families of Individuals with Autism Spectrum Disorder during the COVID-19 Crisis	Manning J, Billian J, Matson J, Allen C, Soares N.	J Autism Dev Disord. 2021 Aug;51(8):2920–2928. doi: 10.1007/s10803-020-04760-5. Epub 2020 Oct 22.	Included in final analysis
34240292[b]	COVID-19 Morbidity among Individuals with Autistic Spectrum Disorder: A Matched Controlled Population-Based Study	Krieger I, Erez G, Weinstein O, Cohen AD, Tzur Bitan D.	J Autism Dev Disord. 2021 Jul 8:1–6. doi: 10.1007/s10803-021-05187-2. Online ahead of print.	Included in the post-survey analysis
34954761[b]	Telehealth Evaluation of Pediatric Neurodevelopmental Disabilities during the COVID-19 Pandemic: Clinician and Caregiver Perspectives	McNally Keehn R, Enneking B, James C, Tang Q, Rouse M, Hines E, Raches C, Etling A.	J Dev Behav Pediatr. 2021 Dec 23. doi: 10.1097/DBP.0000000000001043. Online ahead of print.	Excluded – Did not focus on the experiences of autistics and CODI-19 or their parents
34548878[b]	COVID-19 Vaccination among Individuals with Autism Spectrum Disorder: A Population-Based Study	Weinstein O, Krieger I, Cohen AD, Tzur Bitan D.	Res Autism Spectr Disord. 2021 Nov;89:101865. doi: 10.1016/j.rasd.2021.101865. Epub 2021 Sep 17.	Included in the post-survey analysis
34378858[b]	Feasibility and Acceptability of a Telehealth Model for Autism Diagnostic Evaluations in Children, Adolescents, and Adults	Matthews NL, Skepnek E, Mammen MA, James JS, Malligo A, Lyon A, Mitchell M, Kiefer SL, Smith CJ.	Autism Res. 2021 Dec;14(12):2564–2579. doi: 10.1002/aur.2591. Epub 2021 Aug 11.	Excluded – Study did not focus on the experiences of autistics and COVID-19 or their parents

(Continued)

PubMed ID	Article Title	Author(s)	Citation	Inclusion/Exclusion and Why
34657487[b]	Comparing the Impact of the First and Second Wave of COVID-19 Lockdown on Slovak Families with Typically Developing Children and Children with Autism Spectrum Disorder	Polónyiová K, Belica I, Celušáková H, Janšáková K, Kopčíková M, Szapuová Ž, Ostatníková D.	Autism. 2021 Oct 16: 13623613211051480. doi: 10.1177/13623613211051480. Online ahead of print.	Included in the post-survey analysis
33000394[a]	A Call to Action to Implement Effective COVID-19 Prevention and Screening of Individuals with Severe Intellectual Developmental and Autism Spectrum Disorders	Baghdadli A, Picot MC, Miot S, Munir K.	J Autism Dev Disord. 2021 Jul; 51(7):2566–2568. doi: 10.1007/s10803-020-04719-6.	Excluded – Opinion piece, commentary or letter to the editor
34740217[b]	Hypokalemia-Induced Rhabdomyolysis in a Child with Autism Affected by the COVID-19 Pandemic	Cao LL, Gaffney LK, Marcus C.	J Dev Behav Pediatr. 2021 Nov 3. doi: 10.1097/DBP.0000000000001035. Online ahead of print.	Excluded – Study did not focus on the experiences of autistics and COVID-19 or their parents
34485851[b]	Severe OCD Exacerbation in a Patient with Autism Spectrum Disorder: A Case Report	Gray J, Bazargan-Hejazi S, Ebrahim G, Cho D.	Arch Clin Med Case Rep. 2021;5(3):388–392. doi: 10.26502/acmcr.96550370. Epub 2021 May 5.	Excluded – Study did not focus on the experiences of autistics and COVID-19 or their parents

33387233*[a]	Brief Report: Impact of COVID-19 on Individuals with ASD and Their Caregivers: A Perspective from the SPARK Cohort	White LC, Law JK, Daniels AM, Toroney J, Vernoia B, Xiao S; SPARK Consortium, Feliciano P, Chung WK.	J Autism Dev Disord. 2021 Oct;51(10):3766–3773. doi: 10.1007/s10803-020-04816-6. Epub 2021 Jan 2.	Removed after the fourth step in PRISMA process
32837701[a]	Reopening the Doors to Center-Based ABA Services: Clinical and Safety Protocols during COVID-19	Kornack J, Williams AL, Johnson KA, Mendes EM.	Behav Anal Pract. 2020 Jun 30;13(3):543–549. doi: 10.1007/s40617-020-00462-7. eCollection 2020 Sep.	Excluded – Opinion piece, commentary or letter to the editor
34088351[a]	Sleep Disorders Reveal Distress among Children and Adolescents during the Covid-19 First Wave: Results of A large Web-Based Italian Survey	Dondi A, Fetta A, Lenzi J, Morigi F, Candela E, Rocca A, Cordelli DM, Lanari M.	Ital J Pediatr. 2021 Jun 4;47(1): 130. doi: 10.1186/s13052-021-01083-8.	Excluded – Study did not focus on the experiences of autistics and COVID-19 or their parents
32791524[a]	Introduction to the Special Issue: Addressing Health Disparities in Pediatric Psychology	Valrie C, Thurston I, Santos M.	J Pediatr Psychol. 2020 Sep 1; 45(8):833–838. doi: 10.1093/jpepsy/jsaa066.	Excluded – Study did not focus on the experiences of autistics and COVID-19 or their parents
34591364[b]	Analysis of the SPARK Study COVID-19 Parent Survey: Early Impact of the Pandemic on Access to Services, Child/Parent Mental Health, and Benefits of Online Services	Bhat A.	Autism Res. 2021 Nov;14(11): 2454–2470. doi: 10.1002/aur.2618. Epub 2021 Sep 30.	Included in the post-survey analysis

(Continued)

PubMed ID	Article Title	Author(s)	Citation	Inclusion/Exclusion and Why
32939917[a]	Changes in Access to Educational and Healthcare Services for Individuals with Intellectual and Developmental Disabilities during COVID-19 Restrictions	Jeste S, Hyde C, Distefano C, Halladay A, Ray S, Porath M, Wilson RB, Thurm A.	J Intellect Disabil Res. 2020 Sep 17. doi: 10.1111/jir.12776. Online ahead of print.	Excluded – Opinion piece, commentary or letter to the editor
34512797[b]	Autism Assessment via Telehealth during the Covid 19 Pandemic: Experiences and Perspectives of Autistic adults, Parents/Carers and Clinicians	Gibbs V, Cai RY, Aldridge F, Wong M.	Res Autism Spectr Disord. 2021 Oct;88:101859. doi: 10.1016/ j.rasd.2021.101859. Epub 2021 Sep 6.	Excluded – Study did not focus on the experiences of autistics and COVID-19 or their parents
34827388[b]	A Systematic Review on the Impact of the Social Confinement on People with Autism Spectrum Disorder and Their Caregivers during the COVID-19 Pandemic	Alonso-Esteban Y, López-Ramón MF, Moreno-Campos V, Navarro-Pardo E, Alcantud-Marín F.	Brain Sci. 2021 Oct 22;11(11): 1389. doi: 10.3390/ brainsci11111389.	Included in the post-survey analysis
34548837[b]	Transitioning to Adulthood from Residential Childcare during COVID-19: Experiences of young People with Intellectual Disabilities and/or Autism Spectrum Disorder in South Africa	Mupaku WM, van Breda AD, Kelly B.	Br J Learn Disabil. 2021 Sep; 49(3):341–351. doi: 10.1111/ bld.12409. Epub 2021 Jul 14.	Excluded – Study did not focus on the experiences of autistics and COVID-19 or their parents

32835296[a]	Antipsychotic-Induced Immune Dysfunction: A Consideration for COVID-19 Risk	May M, Slitzky M, Rostama B, Barlow D, Houseknecht KL.	Brain Behav Immun Health. 2020 Jul;6:100097. doi: 10.1016/j.bbih.2020.100097. Epub 2020 Jun 23.	Excluded – Study did not focus on the experiences of autistics and COVID-19 or their parents
35484038[b]	Self-Reported COVID-19 Vaccination Acceptance and Hesitancy among Autistic Adults	Shea LL, Becker A, Lee BK, Miller KK, Cooper D, Anderson K, Salzer MS, Vanness DJ.	Vaccine. 2022 May 26;40(24):3288–3293. doi: 10.1016/j.vaccine.2022.04.060. Epub 2022 Apr 22.	Included in the post-survey analysis
33065268[a]	The Role of Epidemiology in Informing United States Childhood Immunization Policy and Practice	Carter-Pokras O, Hutchins S, Gaudino JA, Veeranki SP, Lurie P, Weiser T, DeMarco M, Khan NF, Cordero JF.	Ann Epidemiol. 2021 Oct;62:100–114. doi: 10.1016/j.annepidem.2020.09.017. Epub 2020 Oct 14.	Excluded – Study did not focus on the experiences of autistics and COVID-19 or their parents
34721108[b]	Impact of the COVID-19 Lockdown in Malaysia: An Examination of the Psychological Well-Being of Parent-Child Dyads and Child Behavior in Families with Children on the Autism Spectrum	Fong HX, Cornish K, Kirk H, Ilias K, Shaikh MF, Golden KJ.	Front Psychiatry. 2021 Oct 14;12:733905. doi: 10.3389/fpsyt.2021.733905. eCollection 2021.	Included in the post-survey analysis
34429669[b]	Parental Self-Efficacy and Behavioral Problems in Children with Autism during COVID-19: A Moderated Mediation Model of Parenting Stress and Perceived Social Support	Chen SD, Yu Y, Li XK, Chen SQ, Ren J.	Psychol Res Behav Manag. 2021 Aug 14;14:1291–1301. doi: 10.2147/PRBM.S327377. eCollection 2021.	Excluded – Study did not focus on the experiences of autistics and COVID-19 or their parents

(*Continued*)

PubMed ID	Article Title	Author(s)	Citation	Inclusion/Exclusion and Why
34276898[b]	Effectiveness of Telehealth Direct Therapy for Individuals with Autism Spectrum Disorder	Nohelty K, Bradford CB, Hirschfeld L, Miyake CJ, Novack MN.	Behav Anal Pract. 2021 Jul 12: 1–16. doi: 10.1007/ s40617-021-00603-6. Online ahead of print.	Excluded – Study did not focus on the experiences of autistics and COVID-19 or their parents
32628369[a]	Supporting Patients with Autism during COVID-19	Yahya AS, Khawaja S.	Prim Care Companion CNS Disord. 2020 Jul 2;22(4): 20com02668. doi: 10.4088/ PCC.20com02668.	Excluded – Opinion piece, commentary or letter to the editor
32545809[a]	Phase 2 and Later of COVID-19 Lockdown: Is it Possible to Perform Remote Diagnosis and Intervention for Autism Spectrum Disorder? An Online-Mediated Approach	Narzisi A.	J Clin Med. 2020 Jun 13;9(6): 1850. doi: 10.3390/ jcm9061850.	Excluded – Study did not focus on the experiences of autistics and COVID-19 or their parents
33648616[a]	The COVID-19 Pandemic Should be Last Orders for Poor Care of People with Neurodevelopmental Disorders	Strydom A, Corcoran E, Rebillat AS.	Br J Psychiatry. 2021 Jun; 218(6):302–304. doi: 10.1192/ bjp.2021.22.	Excluded – Opinion piece, commentary or letter to the editor
34925775[b]	Parents' Perceptions on Physical Activity for their Children with Autism Spectrum Disorders during the Novel Coronavirus Outbreak	Esentürk OK.	Int J Dev Disabil. 2020 May 22; 67(6):446–457. doi: 10.1080/ 20473869.2020.1769333. eCollection 2021.	Included in the post-survey analysis

34666076[b]	SARS-CoV-2-Associated Cytokine Storm during Pregnancy as a Possible Risk Factor for Neuropsychiatric Disorder Development in Post-pandemic Infants	Figueiredo CP, Fontes-Dantas FL, da Poian AT, Clarke JR.	Neuropharmacology. 2021 Dec 15;201:108841. doi: 10.1016/j.neuropharm.2021.108841. Epub 2021 Oct 16.	Excluded – Study did not focus on the experiences of autistics and COVID-19 or their parents
34371305[b]	Autistic Adults' Personal Experiences of Navigating a Social World Prior to and during Covid-19 Lockdown in Spain	Lois Mosquera M, Mandy W, Pavlopoulou G, Dimitriou D.	Res Dev Disabil. 2021 Oct; 117:104057. doi: 10.1016/j.ridd.2021.104057. Epub 2021 Aug 6.	Included in the post-survey analysis
34629580[b]	How Anxiety Predicts Interpersonal Curiosity during the COVID-19 Pandemic: The Mediation Effect of Interpersonal Distancing and Autistic Tendency	Huang Q, Cao S, Zhou S, Punia D, Zhu X, Luo Y, Wu H.	Pers Individ Dif. 2021 Oct;180: 110973. doi: 10.1016/j.paid.2021.110973. Epub 2021 May 18.	Excluded – Study did not focus on the experiences of autistics and COVID-19 or their parents
33535513* [a]	Information and Communication Technologies to Support Early Screening of Autism Spectrum Disorder: A Systematic Review	Desideri L, Pérez-Fuster P, Herrera G.	Children (Basel). 2021 Feb 1; 8(2):93. doi: 10.3390/children8020093.	Removed after the fourth step in PRISMA process
34915925[b]	A Case of Catatonia in the Aftermath of the COVID-19 Pandemic: Does Autism Spectrum Matter?	Dell'Osso L, Amatori G, Gesi C, Carmassi C.	Ann Gen Psychiatry. 2021 Dec 16;20(1):54. doi: 10.1186/s12991-021-00377-9.	Excluded – Study did not focus on the experiences of autistics and COVID-19 or their parents
33540358[a]	Attitude, Anxiety and Perceived Mental Health Care Needs among Parents of Children with Autism Spectrum Disorder (ASD) in Saudi Arabia during COVID-19 Pandemic	Althiabi Y.	Res Dev Disabil. 2021 Apr; 111:103873. doi: 10.1016/j.ridd.2021.103873. Epub 2021 Feb 2.	Included in final analysis

(*Continued*)

PubMed ID	Article Title	Author(s)	Citation	Inclusion/Exclusion and Why
33465589*[a]	While Quarantined: An Online Parent Education and Training Model for Families of Children with Autism in China	McDevitt SE.	Res Dev Disabil. 2021 Feb; 109:103851. doi: 10.1016/ j.ridd.2020.103851. Epub 2021 Jan 16.	Removed after the fourth step in PRISMA process
33600614*[a]	Telehealth Parent Coaching to Improve Daily Living Skills for Children with ASD	Gerow S, Radhakrishnan S, S Akers J, McGinnis K, Swensson R.	J Appl Behav Anal. 2021 Apr; 54(2):566–581. doi: 10.1002/ jaba.813. Epub 2021 Feb 18.	Removed after the fourth step in PRISMA process
34483995[b]	Characterizing Changes in Screen Time during the COVID-19 Pandemic School Closures in Canada and Its Perceived Impact on Children with Autism Spectrum Disorder	Cardy RE, Dupuis A, Anagnostou E, Ziolkowski J, Biddiss EA, Monga S, Brian J, Penner M, Kushki A.	Front Psychiatry. 2021 Aug 18; 12:702774. doi: 10.3389/ fpsyt.2021.702774. eCollection 2021.	Excluded – Study did not focus on the experiences of autistics and COVID-19 or their parents
34327131[b]	Mental Health of Parents of Children with Autism Spectrum Disorder during COVID-19 Pandemic: A Systematic Review	Yılmaz B, Azak M, Şahin N.	World J Psychiatry. 2021 Jul 19;11(7):388–402. doi: 10.5498/wjp.v11.i7.388. eCollection 2021 Jul 19.	Included in the post-survey analysis
34670768[b]	Psychological Burden of Attention-Deficit/Hyperactivity Disorder Traits on Medical Workers Under the COVID-19 Outbreak: A Cross-Sectional Web-Based Questionnaire Survey	Matsui K, Yoshiike T, Tsuru A, Otsuki R, Nagao K, Ayabe N, Hazumi M, Utsumi T, Yamamoto K, Fukumizu M, Kuriyama K.	BMJ Open. 2021 Oct 20; 11(10):e053737. doi: 10.1136/ bmjopen-2021-053737.	Excluded – Study did not focus on the experiences of autistics and COVID-19 or their parents

33765076[a]	Remote Assessment in Adults with Autism or ADHD: A Service User Satisfaction Survey	Adamou M, Jones SL, Fullen T, Galab N, Abbott K, Yasmeen S.	PLoS One. 2021 Mar 25;16(3): e0249237. doi: 10.1371/journal.pone.0249237. eCollection 2021.	Excluded – Study did not focus on the experiences of autistics and COVID-19 or their parents
34262486[b]	Leveraging Technology for the Wellbeing of Individuals with Autism Spectrum Disorder and Their Families during Covid-19	Doenyas C, Shohieb SM.	Front Psychiatry. 2021 Jun 28; 12:566809. doi: 10.3389/fpsyt.2021.566809. eCollection 2021.	Excluded – Opinion piece, commentary or letter to the editor
34087907[a]	COVID-19 Phobia in a Boy with Undiagnosed Autism Spectrum Disorder: A Case Report	Sakamoto S, Miyawaki D, Goto A, Harima Y, Tokuhara D, Inoue K.	Medicine (Baltimore). 2021 Jun 4;100(22):e26233. doi: 10.1097/MD.0000000000026233.	Excluded – Case study
34118499[a]	Addressing Pediatric Mental Health Using Telehealth during Coronavirus Disease-2019 and Beyond: A Narrative Review	Cunningham NR, Ely SL, Barber Garcia BN, Bowden J.	Acad Pediatr. 2021 Sep-Oct; 21(7):1108–1117. doi: 10.1016/j.acap.2021.06.002. Epub 2021 Jun 9.	Excluded – Opinion piece, commentary or letter to the editor
33556700* [a]	A Parent-Sibling Dyadic Interview to Explore How an Individual with Autism Spectrum Disorder can Impact Family Dynamics	Critchley E, Cuadros M, Harper I, Smith-Howell H, Rogish M.	Res Dev Disabil. 2021 Apr; 111:103884. doi: 10.1016/j.ridd.2021.103884. Epub 2021 Feb 5.	Removed after the fourth step in PRISMA process
34997196[b]	Mechanisms of Action of Fluvoxamine for COVID-19: A Historical review	Hashimoto Y, Suzuki T, Hashimoto K.	Mol Psychiatry. 2022 Apr; 27(4):1898–1907. doi: 10.1038/s41380-021-01432-3. Epub 2022 Jan 7.	Excluded – Study did not focus on the experiences of autistics and COVID-19 or their parents

(*Continued*)

PubMed ID	Article Title	Author(s)	Citation	Inclusion/Exclusion and Why
33031918[a]	Understanding the Genetic Contribution of the Human Leukocyte Antigen System to Common Major Psychiatric Disorders in a World Pandemic Context	Tamouza R, Krishnamoorthy R, Leboyer M.	Brain Behav Immun. 2021 Jan; 91:731–739. doi: 10.1016/ j.bbi.2020.09.033. Epub 2020 Oct 5.	Excluded – Study did not focus on the experiences of autistics and COVID-19 or their parents
33897973* [a]	Developing Remote Delivery of Language and Cognitive Training for Use with Children with Autism: A Technological Report	Belisle J, Burke R, Clark L, Jepsen R, Welch K, Dennis L, McDonald N.	Behav Anal Pract. 2021 Apr 20;14(2):434–444. doi: 10.1007/s40617-020-00544-6. eCollection 2021 Jun.	Removed after the fourth step in PRISMA process
33540683* [a]	The Impact of COVID-19 on the Adaptive Functioning, Behavioral Problems, and Repetitive Behaviors of Italian Children with Autism Spectrum Disorder: An Observational Study	Siracusano M, Segatori E, Riccioni A, Emberti Gialloreti L, Curatolo P, Mazzone L.	Children (Basel). 2021 Feb 2; 8(2):96. doi: 10.3390/ children8020096.	Removed after the fourth step in PRISMA process
33689088[a]	COVID-19 Pandemic and Impact on Patients with Autism Spectrum Disorder	Baweja R, Brown SL, Edwards EM, Murray MJ.	J Autism Dev Disord. 2022 Jan;52(1):473–482. doi: 10.1007/s10803-021-04950-9. Epub 2021 Mar 10.	Excluded – Opinion piece, commentary or letter to the editor
33241588[a]	Telehealth Mask Wearing Training for Children with Autism during the COVID-19 Pandemic	Sivaraman M, Virues-Ortega J, Roeyers H.	J Appl Behav Anal. 2021 Jan; 54(1):70–86. doi: 10.1002/ jaba.802. Epub 2020 Nov 25.	Removed in the fourth step in PRISMA process

33909902[a]	A Hybrid Clinical Trial Delivery Model in the COVID-19 Era	Bhat A, Su WC, Cleffi C, Srinivasan S.	Phys Ther. 2021 Aug 1;101(8): pzab116. doi: 10.1093/ptj/pzab116.	Excluded – Study did not focus on the experiences of autistics and COVID-19 or their parents
34912192[b]	Systemic Inflammation and Astrocyte Reactivity in the Neuropsychiatric Sequelae of COVID-19: Focus on Autism Spectrum Disorders	Valenza M, Steardo L Jr, Steardo L, Verkhratsky A, Scuderi C.	Front Cell Neurosci. 2021 Nov 29;15:748136. doi: 10.3389/fncel.2021.748136. eCollection 2021.	Excluded – Study did not focus on the experiences of autistics and COVID-19 or their parents
33551857* [a]	The Resilience of Social Service Providers and Families of Children with Autism or Development Delays during the COVID-19 Pandemic-A Community Case Study in Hong Kong	Wong PW, Lam Y, Lau JS, Fok H.	Front Psychiatry. 2021 Jan 22; 11:561657. doi: 10.3389/fpsyt.2020.561657. eCollection 2020.	Removed after the fourth step in PRISMA process
33125622* [a]	Use of the TELE-ASD-PEDS for Autism Evaluations in Response to COVID-19: Preliminary Outcomes and Clinician Acceptability	Wagner L, Corona LL, Weitlauf AS, Marsh KL, Berman AF, Broderick NA, Francis S, Hine J, Nicholson A, Stone C, Warren Z.	J Autism Dev Disord. 2021 Sep;51(9):3063–3072. doi: 10.1007/s10803-020-04767-y. Epub 2020 Oct 30.	Removed after the fourth step in PRISMA process
34591895[b]	Facial Masks Affect Emotion Recognition in the General Population and Individuals with Autistic Traits	Pazhoohi F, Forby L, Kingstone A.	PLoS One. 2021 Sep 30;16(9): e0257740. doi: 10.1371/journal.pone.0257740. eCollection 2021.	Included in the post-survey analysis

(*Continued*)

PubMed ID	Article Title	Author(s)	Citation	Inclusion/Exclusion and Why
32413984[a]	Should Autism Spectrum Conditions Be Characterised in a More Positive Way in Our Modern World?	Wright B, Spikins P, Pearson H.	Medicina (Kaunas). 2020 May 13;56(5):233. doi: 10.3390/medicina56050233.	Excluded – Opinion piece, commentary or letter to the editor
33657458[a]	Autism Spectrum Disorder Patients may be Susceptible to COVID-19 Disease due to Deficiency in Melatonin	Brown GM, Karthikeyan R, Pandi-Perumal SR, Cardinali DP.	Med Hypotheses. 2021 Apr; 149:110544. doi: 10.1016/j.mehy.2021.110544. Epub 2021 Feb 18.	Excluded – Opinion piece, commentary or letter to the editor
34988286[b]	ECHO Autism: Evaluation of Participants' Perceptions of Collaborative Telementoring Network	Becevic M, Nair P, Wallach E, Hoffman K, Sohl K.	J Patient Exp. 2021 Dec 20;8: 23743735211065292. doi: 10.1177/23743735211065292. eCollection 2021.	Excluded – Study did not focus on the experiences of autistics and COVID-19 or their parents
34386166[b]	Challenges in managing children with Autism Spectrum Disorder and COVID-19: A Case Report	Shaji G, Chong VH.	Malays Fam Physician. 2021 May 31;16(2):67–69. doi: 10.51866/cr1137. eCollection 2021 Jul 22.	Excluded – Study did not focus on the experiences of autistics and COVID-19 or their parents
34666575[b]	Barriers Leading to Increased Disability in Neurologically Challenged Populations during COVID-19 Pandemic: A Scoping Review	D'souza J, Biswas A, Gada P, Mangroliya J, Natarajan M.	Disabil Rehabil. 2021 Oct 19: 1–14. doi: 10.1080/09638288.2021.1986747. Online ahead of print.	Excluded – Study did not focus on the experiences of autistics and COVID-19 or their parents

33385281[a]	Conducting CBT for Anxiety in Children with Autism Spectrum Disorder during COVID-19 Pandemic	Kalvin CB, Jordan RP, Rowley SN, Weis A, Wood KS, Wood JJ, Ibrahim K, Sukhodolsky DG.	J Autism Dev Disord. 2021 Nov;51(11):4239–4247. doi: 10.1007/s10803-020-04845-1. Epub 2021 Jan 1.	Excluded – Opinion piece, commentary or letter to the editor
34449147[b]	Effects of Lockdown during Corona Pandemic on Children with Neurodevelopmental Disorders-A Questionnaire-Based Survey	Goswami JN, Sondhi V, Simalti AK, Bamal M, Roy S.	Turk J Pediatr. 2021;63(4): 648–659. doi: 10.24953/turkjped.2021.04.012.	Excluded – Study did not focus on the experiences of autistics and COVID-19 or their parents
33490369[a]	Real-Time Telehealth Treatment Team Consultation for Self-Injury by Individuals with Autism Spectrum Disorder	Singh NN, Lancioni GE, Medvedev ON, Hwang YS, Myers RE.	Adv Neurodev Disord. 2021; 5(2):170–182. doi: 10.1007/s41252-021-00192-z. Epub 2021 Jan 19.	Excluded – Did not focus on the experiences of autistics and COVID-19 or their parents
34192189[a]	Scoping Exercise to Develop a Storybook to Support Children's Education during the COVID-19 Pandemic	Syeda R, Hann M, Allison R, Demirjian A.	BMJ Paediatr Open. 2021 Mar 4;5(1):e000926. doi: 10.1136/bmjpo-2020-000926. eCollection 2021.	Excluded – Did not focus on the experiences of autistics and COVID-19 or their parents
32851355[a]	Prospects for Improving Future Mental Health of Children Through Prenatal Maternal Micronutrient Supplementation in China	Li Y, Freedman R.	Pediatr Investig. 2020 Jun 24; 4(2):118–126. doi: 10.1002/ped4.12199. eCollection 2020 Jun.	Excluded – Study did not focus on the experiences of autistics and COVID-19 or their parents
33221246[a]	Brief Report: The Impact of the COVID-19 Pandemic on Health Behaviors in Adolescents with Autism Spectrum Disorder	Garcia JM, Lawrence S, Brazendale K, Leahy N, Fukuda D.	Disabil Health J. 2021 Apr; 14(2):101021. doi: 10.1016/j.dhjo.2020.101021. Epub 2020 Nov 5.	Included in final analysis

(*Continued*)

PubMed ID	Article Title	Author(s)	Citation	Inclusion/Exclusion and Why
34914016[b]	The Brief Observation of Symptoms of Autism (BOSA): Development of a New Adapted Assessment Measure for Remote Telehealth Administration Through COVID-19 and Beyond	Dow D, Holbrook A, Toolan C, McDonald N, Sterrett K, Rosen N, Kim SH, Lord C.	J Autism Dev Disord. 2021 Dec 16:1–12. doi: 10.1007/s10803-021-05395-w. Online ahead of print.	Excluded – Study did not focus on the experiences of autistics and COVID-19 or their parents
34611836[b]	Brief Report: Feasibility and Acceptability of a Remote-Based Nutrition Education Program for Adolescents with Autism Spectrum Disorder: A COVID-19 Pilot Study	Shurack RH, Garcia JM, Brazendale K, Lee E.	J Autism Dev Disord. 2021 Oct 5:1–7. doi: 10.1007/s10803-021-05301-4. Online ahead of print.	Included in the post-survey analysis
34575637[b]	Ways to Address Perinatal Mast Cell Activation and Focal Brain Inflammation, including Response to SARS-CoV-2, in Autism Spectrum Disorder	Theoharides TC.	J Pers Med. 2021 Aug 29; 11(9):860. doi: 10.3390/jpm11090860.	Excluded – Study did not focus on the experiences of autistics and COVID-19 or their parents
34363330[b]	Psychological Distress among Caregivers Raising a Child with Autism Spectrum Disorder during the COVID-19 Pandemic	Kalb LG, Badillo-Goicoechea E, Holingue C, Riehm KE, Thrul J, Stuart EA, Smail EJ, Law K, White-Lehman C, Fallin D.	Autism Res. 2021 Oct;14(10): 2183–2188. doi: 10.1002/aur.2589. Epub 2021 Aug 7.	Included in the post-survey analysis

34426842[b]	Prioritization of Persons with Special Needs in Covid-19 Vaccinations in the Philippines	Maboloc CR.	J Public Health (Oxf). 2021 Aug 23:fdab324. doi: 10.1093/pubmed/fdab324. Online ahead of print.	Excluded – Opinion piece, commentary or letter to the editor
34236591[b]	Factors Contributing to Psychological Ill-Effects and Resilience of Caregivers of Children with Developmental Disabilities during a Nation-wide Lockdown during the COVID-19 Pandemic	Lim TSH, Tan MY, Aishworiya R, Kang YQ, Koh MY, Shen L, Chong SC.	J Autism Dev Disord. 2021 Jul 8:1–11. doi: 10.1007/s10803-021-05180-9. Online ahead of print.	Excluded – Study did not focus on the experiences of autistics and COVID-19 or their parents
34679621[b]	Features of Mobile Apps for People with Autism in a Post COVID-19 Scenario: Current Status and Recommendations for Apps Using AI	Rehman IU, Sobnath D, Nasralla MM, Winnett M, Anwar A, Asif W, Sherazi HHR.	Diagnostics (Basel). 2021 Oct 17;11(10):1923. doi: 10.3390/diagnostics11101923.	Excluded – Opinion piece, commentary or letter to the editor
34362263[b]	COVID-19, Social Isolation and the Mental Health of Autistic People and their Families: A Qualitative Study	Pellicano E, Brett S, den Houting J, Heyworth M, Magiati I, Steward R, Urbanowicz A, Stears M.	Autism. 2022 May;26(4):914–927. doi: 10.1177/13623613211035936. Epub 2021 Aug 6.	Included in the post-survey analysis
34831567[b]	Practitioner and Service User Perspectives on the Rapid Shift to Teletherapy for Individuals on the Autism Spectrum as a Result of COVID-19	Johnsson G, Bulkeley K.	Int J Environ Res Public Health. 2021 Nov 11;18(22):11812. doi: 10.3390/ijerph182211812.	Excluded – Study did not focus on the experiences of autistics and COVID-19 or their parents

(*Continued*)

PubMed ID	Article Title	Author(s)	Citation	Inclusion/Exclusion and Why
34462727[b]	Evaluation of a Pilot Healthy Eating and Exercise Program for Young Adults with Autism Spectrum Disorder and Intellectual Disabilities	Nabors L, Overstreet A, Carnahan C, Ayers K.	Adv Neurodev Disord. 2021; 5(4):413–430. doi: 10.1007/s41252-021-00214-w. Epub 2021 Aug 25.	Excluded – Study did not focus on the experiences of autistics and COVID-19 or their parents
33484052[a]	'It's Been adapted Rather than Impacted': A Qualitative Evaluation of the Impact of Covid-19 Restrictions on the Positive Behavioural Support of People with an Intellectual Disability and/or Autism	McKenzie K, Murray GC, Martin R.	J Appl Res Intellect Disabil. 2021 Jul;34(4):1089–1097. doi: 10.1111/jar.12859. Epub 2021 Jan 22.	Excluded – Study did not focus on the experiences of autistics and COVID-19 or their parents
33350655[a]	Use of Telehealth in Fellowship-Affiliated Developmental Behavioral Pediatric Practices during the COVID-19 Pandemic	Wallis KE, Mulé C, Mittal S, Cerda N, Shaffer R, Scott A, Langkamp D, Augustyn M, Perrin E, Soares N, Blum NJ.	J Dev Behav Pediatr. 2021 May 1;42(4):314–321. doi: 10.1097/DBP.0000000000000897.	Excluded – Study did not focus on the experiences of autistics and COVID-19 or their parents
33163146* [a]	Developing and Enhancing Adherence to a Telehealth ABA Parent Training Curriculum for Caregivers of Children with Autism	Yi Z, Dixon MR.	Behav Anal Pract. 2020 Nov 3; 14(1):58–74. doi: 10.1007/s40617-020-00464-5. eCollection 2021 Mar.	Removed after the fourth step in PRISMA process

35132414[b]	SARS-CoV-2 Invades Cognitive Centers of the Brain and Induces Alzheimer's-Like Neuropathology	Shen WB, Logue J, Yang P, Baracco L, Elahi M, Reece EA, Wang B, Li L, Blanchard TG, Han Z, Frieman MB, Rissman RA, Yang P.	bioRxiv. 2022 Feb 3: 2022.01.31.478476. doi: 10.1101/ 2022.01.31.478476. Preprint.	Excluded – Study did not focus on the experiences of autistics and COVID-19 or their parents
34939747[b]	Experiences of Student and Trainee Autism Researchers during the COVID-19 Pandemic	Kaku SM, McVey AJ, Gerber AH, Pretzsch CM, Jones DR, Kodakkadan FM, Lei J, Singer L, Chitehwe L, Poulsen RE, Coffman M.	Autism Res. 2022 Mar;15(3): 413–420. doi: 10.1002/ aur.2662. Epub 2021 Dec 23.	Excluded – Study did not focus on the experiences of autistics and COVID-19 or their parents
34207173* [a]	Psychological Impact of COVID-19 Outbreak on Families of Children with Autism Spectrum Disorder and Typically Developing Peers: An Online Survey	Levante A, Petrocchi S, Bianco F, Castelli I, Colombi C, Keller R, Narzisi A, Masi G, Lecciso F.	Brain Sci. 2021 Jun 18;11(6): 808. doi: 10.3390/ brainsci11060808.	Removed after the fourth step in PRISMA process
33882385* [a]	Home Education for Children with Autism Spectrum Disorder during the COVID-19 Pandemic: Indonesian Mothers Experience	Daulay N.	Res Dev Disabil. 2021 Jul;114: 103954. doi: 10.1016/ j.ridd.2021.103954. Epub 2021 Apr 5.	Removed after the fourth step in PRISMA process
35078834[b]	Impact of the COVID-19 Pandemic on Children and Adolescents with Autism Spectrum Disorder and their Families: A mixed-Methods Study Protocol	Dekker L, Hooijman L, Louwerse A, Visser K, Bastiaansen D, Ten Hoopen L, De Nijs P, Dieleman G, Ester W, Van Rijen S, Truijens F, Van der Hallen R.	BMJ Open. 2022 Jan 25;12(1): e049336. doi: 10.1136/ bmjopen-2021-049336.	Included in the post-survey analysis

(*Continued*)

PubMed ID	Article Title	Author(s)	Citation	Inclusion/Exclusion and Why
35077878[b]	Severe Outcomes, Readmission, and Length of Stay among COVID-19 Patients with Intellectual and Developmental Disabilities	Koyama AK, Koumans EH, Sircar K, Lavery A, Hsu J, Ryerson AB, Siegel DA.	Int J Infect Dis. 2022 Mar;116: 328–330. doi: 10.1016/j.ijid.2022.01.038. Epub 2022 Jan 22.	Excluded – Study did not focus on the experiences of autistics and COVID-19 or their parents
34865678[b]	COVID-19 Pandemic Impact on Psychotropic Prescribing for Adults with Intellectual Disability: An Observational Study in English Specialist Community Services	Naqvi D, Perera B, Mitchell S, Sheehan R, Shankar R.	BJPsych Open. 2021 Dec 6; 8(1):e7. doi: 10.1192/bjo.2021.1064.	Excluded – Study did not focus on the experiences of autistics and COVID-19 or their parents
34124631[a]	A Media Intervention Applying Debunking Versus Non-debunking Content to Combat Vaccine Misinformation in Elderly in the Netherlands: A Digital Randomised Trial	Yousuf H, van der Linden S, Bredius L, Ted van Essen GA, Sweep G, Preminger Z, van Gorp E, Scherder E, Narula J, Hofstra L.	EClinicalMedicine. 2021 May 15;35:100881. doi: 10.1016/j.eclinm.2021.100881. eCollection 2021 May.	Excluded – Study did not focus on the experiences of autistics and COVID-19 or their parents
34002690[a]	Revisiting Vitamin D Status and Supplementation for In-patients with Intellectual and Developmental Disability in the North of England, UK	Dudley B, Ostrowski M, Ciausu V, Ince C, McKinnon I.	BJPsych Bull. 2021 May 18: 1–7. doi: 10.1192/bjb.2021.55. Online ahead of print.	Excluded – Study did not focus on the experiences of autistics and COVID-19 or their parents

34996019[b]	The Myth of Vaccination and Autism Spectrum	Gabis LV, Attia OL, Goldman M, Barak N, Tefera P, Shefer S, Shaham M, Lerman-Sagie T.	Eur J Paediatr Neurol. 2022 Jan;36:151–158. doi: 10.1016/j.ejpn.2021.12.011. Epub 2021 Dec 22.	Excluded – Study did not focus on the experiences of autistics and COVID-19 or their parents
33935477[a]	Naturalistic Communication Training for Early Intervention Providers and Latinx Parents of Children with Signs of Autism	Gevarter C, Najar AM, Flake J, Tapia-Alvidrez F, Lucero A.	J Dev Phys Disabil. 2021 Apr 28:1–23. doi: 10.1007/s10882-021-09794-w. Online ahead of print.	Excluded – Study did not focus on the experiences of autistics and COVID-19 or their parents
35455891[b]	Psychosocial and Behavioral Effects of the COVID-19 Pandemic on Children and Adolescents with Autism and Their Families: Overview of the Literature and Initial Data from a Multinational Online Survey	Kreysa H, Schneider D, Kowallik AE, Dastgheib SS, Doğdu C, Kühn G, Ruttloff JM, Schweinberger SR.	Healthcare (Basel). 2022 Apr 12;10(4):714. doi: 10.3390/healthcare10040714.	Included in the post-survey analysis
34421194[b]	Examination of the Effectiveness and Acceptability of a Play-Based Sibling Intervention for Children with Autism: A Single-Case Research Design	Glugatch LB, Machalicek W.	Educ Treat Children. 2021; 44(4):249–267. doi: 10.1007/s43494-021-00043-5. Epub 2021 Aug 16.	Excluded – Study did not focus on the experiences of autistics and COVID-19 or their parents
33560019[a]	Future Perspectives of Robot Psychiatry: Can Communication Robots Assist Psychiatric Evaluation in the COVID-19 Pandemic Era?	Yoshikawa Y, Kumazaki H, Kato TA.	Curr Opin Psychiatry. 2021 May 1;34(3):277–286. doi: 10.1097/YCO.0000000000000692.	Excluded – Study did not focus on the experiences of autistics and COVID-19 or their parents

(*Continued*)

PubMed ID	Article Title	Author(s)	Citation	Inclusion/Exclusion and Why
35620553[b]	Mental Health Impacts of the COVID-19 Pandemic on Children with Underlying Health and Disability Issues, and their Families and Health Care Providers	Nicholas DB, Zulla RT, Conlon O, Dimitropoulos G, Urschel S, Rapoport A, Katz SL, Bruce A, West LJ, Belletrutti M, Cullen E, Zwaigenbaum L.	Paediatr Child Health. 2022 May 9;27(Suppl 1):S33–S39. doi: 10.1093/pch/pxab103. eCollection 2022 Jun.	Excluded – Study did not focus on the experiences of autistics and COVID-19 or their parents
35046876[b]	Burnt Out and Dropping Out: A Comparison of the Experiences of Autistic and Non-autistic Students during the COVID-19 Pandemic	Cage E, McManemy E.	Front Psychol. 2022 Jan 3;12: 792945. doi: 10.3389/ fpsyg.2021.792945. eCollection 2021.	Included in the post-survey analysis
34849195[b]	A k-mer based Approach for Classifying Viruses Without Taxonomy Identifies Viral Associations in Human Autism and Plant Microbiomes	Garcia BJ, Simha R, Garvin M, Furches A, Jones P, Gazolla JGFM, Hyatt PD, Schadt CW, Pelletier D, Jacobson D.	Comput Struct Biotechnol J. 2021 Oct 25;19:5911–5919. doi: 10.1016/ j.csbj.2021.10.029. eCollection 2021.	Excluded – Study did not focus on the experiences of autistics and COVID-19 or their parents
34183470[a]	Autism Spectrum Disorder in the COVID 19 Era: New Challenges – New Solutions	Bharat R, Uzaina -, Niranjan S, Yadav T, Newman S, Marriott J, Smith G, Sawlani G.	Indian Pediatr. 2021 Sep 15; 58(9):888–889. Epub 2021 Jun 28.	Excluded – Article could not be accessed

33159508[a]	Transforming Pediatric Neuropsychology Through Video-Based Teleneuropsychology: An Innovative Private Practice Model pre-COVID-19	Salinas CM, Bordes Edgar V, Berrios Siervo G, Bender HA.	Arch Clin Neuropsychol. 2020 Nov 19;35(8):1189–1195. doi: 10.1093/arclin/acaa101.	Excluded – Study did not focus on the experiences of autistics and COVID-19 or their parents
34525940[b]	Utilization of Telemedicine to Support Caregivers of Young Children with ASD and their Part C Service Providers: A Comparison of Intervention Outcomes Across Three Models of Service Delivery	Corona LL, Stainbrook JA, Simcoe K, Wagner L, Fowler B, Weitlauf AS, Juárez AP, Warren Z.	J Neurodev Disord. 2021 Sep 15;13(1):38. doi: 10.1186/s11689-021-09387-w.	Excluded – Study did not focus on the experiences of autistics and COVID-19 or their parents
34533658[b]	Adults with Autism Should be Considered a Priority in COVID-19 Immunization Programs	Lucena R, de Melo-Carneiro P, Sampaio AS, de Almeida NR, Ponte AMV, de Brito Wanderley D, de Mattos AM, Robatto AP, Argollo N.	J Autism Dev Disord. 2021 Sep 17:1–2. doi: 10.1007/s10803-021-05281-5. Online ahead of print.	Excluded – Opinion piece, commentary or letter to the editor
33059534[a]	'How to' Operate a Pediatric Neuropsychology Practice during the COVID-19 Pandemic: Real tips from One Practice's Experience	Loman M, Vogt E, Miller L, Landsman R, Duong P, Kasten J, DeFrancisco D, Koop J, Heffelfinger A.	Child Neuropsychol. 2021 Feb;27(2):251–279. doi: 10.1080/09297049.2020.1830962. Epub 2020 Oct 16.	Excluded – Opinion piece, commentary or letter to the editor
32746638[a]	The Relationship between Chronotype, Sleep, and Autism Symptom Severity in Children with ASD in COVID-19 Home Confinement Period	Türkoğlu S, Uçar HN, Çetin FH, Güler HA, Tezcan ME.	Chronobiol Int. 2020 Aug;37(8):1207–1213. doi: 10.1080/07420528.2020.1792485. Epub 2020 Aug 4.	Included in final analysis

(*Continued*)

PubMed ID	Article Title	Author(s)	Citation	Inclusion/Exclusion and Why
35416566[b]	The COVID-19 Pandemic and its Impact on tic Symptoms in Children and Young People: A Prospective Cohort Study	Hall CL, Marston L, Khan K, Brown BJ, Sanderson C, Andrén P, Bennett S, Heyman I, Mataix-Cols D, Serlachius E, Hollis C, Murphy T.	Child Psychiatry Hum Dev. 2022 Apr 13:1–11. doi: 10.1007/s10578-022-01348-1. Online ahead of print.	Excluded – Study did not focus on the experiences of autistics and COVID-19 or their parents
33569014* [a]	Enhancing Communication Skills of Individuals with Autism Spectrum Disorders While Maintaining Social Distancing Using Two Tele-Operated Robots	Kumazaki H, Muramatsu T, Yoshikawa Y, Haraguchi H, Sono T, Matsumoto Y, Ishiguro H, Kikuchi M, Sumiyoshi T, Mimura M.	Front Psychiatry. 2021 Jan 25; 11:598688. doi: 10.3389/fpsyt.2020.598688. eCollection 2020.	Removed after the fourth step in PRISMA process
33536883[a]	Digging Signatures in 13-Month-Old 3xTg-AD Mice for Alzheimer's Disease and Its Disruption by Isolation Despite Social Life Since They Were Born	Gimenez-Llort L, Alveal-Mellado D.	Front Behav Neurosci. 2021 Jan 18;14:611384. doi: 10.3389/fnbeh.2020.611384. eCollection 2020.	Excluded – Study did not focus on the experiences of autistics and COVID-19 or their parents
34238041[b]	Update on Neurodegenerative Diseases and Glutamate: A PMHNP Single Case Study Report of a Diagnostically Complex Adult Patient, Interventions, and Unexpected Outcomes	Kroll SC, Bennett CF, Klinefelter TW.	J Am Psychiatr Nurses Assoc. 2021 Jul 8: 10783903211030343. doi: 10.1177/10783903211030343. Online ahead of print.	Excluded – Study did not focus on the experiences of autistics and COVID-19 or their parents

33481751* [a]	The Efficacy of WeChat-Based Parenting Training on the Psychological Well-being of Mothers with Children with Autism during the COVID-19 Pandemic: Quasi-Experimental Study	Liu G, Wang S, Liao J, Ou P, Huang L, Xie N, He Y, Lin J, He HG, Hu R.	JMIR Ment Health. 2021 Feb 10;8(2):e23917. doi: 10.2196/23917.	Removed after the fourth step in PRISMA process
34104925[a]	The Impact of the COVID-19 Pandemic on the Assessment of Autism Spectrum Disorder	Posar A, Visconti P, Giuberti V.	Turk Arch Pediatr. 2021 May 1; 56(3):280–282. doi: 10.5152/ TurkArchPediatr.2021.20269. eCollection 2021.	Excluded – Opinion piece, commentary or letter to the editor
32244776[a]	Handle the Autism Spectrum Condition during Coronavirus (COVID-19) Stay At Home period: Ten Tips for Helping Parents and Caregivers of Young Children	Narzisi A.	Brain Sci. 2020 Apr 1;10(4): 207. doi: 10.3390/ brainsci10040207.	Excluded – Opinion piece, commentary or letter to the editor
32826708[a]	Far from an Elective Procedure: Electroconvulsive Therapy and Autism in the Era of COVID-19	Wachtel LE.	J ECT. 2021 Mar 1;37(1): 10–12. doi: 10.1097/ YCT.0000000000000720.	Excluded – Opinion piece, commentary or letter to the editor
35455091[b]	Changes in the Mean of Medical Visits Due to Psychiatric Disease in Korean Children and Adolescents before and during the COVID-19 Pandemic	Kim SY, Lee NE, Yoo DM, Kim JH, Kwon MJ, Kim JH, Bang WJ, Choi HG.	Life (Basel). 2022 Apr 18;12(4): 600. doi: 10.3390/ life12040600.	Excluded – Study did not focus on the experiences of autistics and COVID-19 or their parents

(*Continued*)

PubMed ID	Article Title	Author(s)	Citation	Inclusion/Exclusion and Why
32715636[a]	The Impact of COVID-19 on Autism Research: Reflections from China	Wang C.	Autism Res. 2020 Jul;13(7): 1028. doi: 10.1002/aur.2344.	Excluded – Opinion piece, commentary or letter to the editor
34173514[a]	Considering Covid-19: Autoethnographic Reflections on Working Practices in a Time of Crisis by Two Disabled UK Academics	Hannam-Swain S, Bailey C.	Soc Sci Humanit Open. 2021; 4(1):100145. doi: 10.1016/ j.ssaho.2021.100145. Epub 2021 Mar 26.	Excluded – Opinion piece, commentary or letter to the editor
34954508[b]	SYNGAP1-Related Developmental and Epileptic Encephalopathy: The Impact on Daily Life	Lo Barco T, De Gaetano L, Santangelo E, Bravi T, Proietti J, Cantalupo G, Brambilla I, Darra F.	Epilepsy Behav. 2022 Feb; 127:108500. doi: 10.1016/ j.yebeh.2021.108500. Epub 2021 Dec 23.	Excluded – Study did not focus on the experiences of autistics and COVID-19 or their parents
34216816[b]	Promoting Physical Activity Participation and Nutrition Education Through a Telehealth Intervention for Children on the Autism Spectrum and Their Caregivers	Ketcheson LR, Pitchford EA.	Contemp Clin Trials. 2021 Aug;107:106496. doi: 10.1016/j.cct.2021.106496. Epub 2021 Jul 1.	Excluded – Study did not focus on the experiences of autistics and COVID-19 or their parents
35143494[b]	A Scoping Review of Telehealth Diagnosis of Autism Spectrum Disorder	Stavropoulos KK, Bolourian Y, Blacher J.	PLoS One. 2022 Feb 10;17(2): e0263062. doi: 10.1371/ journal.pone.0263062. eCollection 2022.	Excluded – Study did not focus on the experiences of autistics and COVID-19 or their parents

33984092[a]	Cardiogenic Shock due to COVID-19-Related Myocarditis in a 19-Year-Old Autistic Patient	Pascariello G, Cimino G, Calvi E, Bernardi N, Grigolato M, Garyfallidis P, Fabbricatore D, Pezzola E, Lombardi CM, Metra M, Vizzardi E.	J Med Cases. 2020 Jul;11(7): 207–210. doi: 10.14740/jmc3517. Epub 2020 Jun 29.	Excluded – Case study
35615409[b]	Mental Health Profiles of Autistic Children and Youth during the COVID-19 Pandemic	Charalampopoulou M, Choi EJ, Korczak DJ, Cost KT, Crosbie J, Birken CS, Charach A, Monga S, Kelley E, Nicolson R, Georgiades S, Ayub M, Schachar RJ, Iaboni A, Anagnostou E.	Paediatr Child Health. 2022 May 5;27(Suppl 1):S59–S65. doi: 10.1093/pch/pxab111. eCollection 2022 Jun.	Included in the post-survey analysis
33641028[a]	Factors Affecting the Behavior of Children with ASD during the First Outbreak of the COVID-19 Pandemic	Nuñez A, Le Roy C, Coelho-Medeiros ME, López-Espejo M.	Neurol Sci. 2021 May;42(5): 1675–1678. doi: 10.1007/s10072-021-05147-9. Epub 2021 Feb 28.	Included in final analysis
34444263[b]	Behavioural Improvements in Children with Autism Spectrum Disorder After Participation in an Adapted Judo Programme Followed by Deleterious Effects during the COVID-19 Lockdown	Morales J, Fukuda DH, Garcia V, Pierantozzi E, Curto C, Martínez-Ferrer JO, Gómez AM, Carballeira E, Guerra-Balic M.	Int J Environ Res Public Health. 2021 Aug 12;18(16): 8515. doi: 10.3390/ijerph18168515.	Included in the post-survey analysis
34191764[a]	COVID-19 Pandemic Highlights Access Barriers for Children with Autism Spectrum Disorder	McNally Keehn R, Tomlin A, Ciccarelli MR.	J Dev Behav Pediatr. 2021 Sep 1;42(7):599–601. doi: 10.1097/DBP.0000000000000988.	Excluded – Opinion piece, commentary or letter to the editor

(*Continued*)

PubMed ID	Article Title	Author(s)	Citation	Inclusion/Exclusion and Why
33353165[a]	Mental Health of Parents of Special Needs Children in China during the COVID-19 Pandemic	Chen SQ, Chen SD, Li XK, Ren J.	Int J Environ Res Public Health. 2020 Dec 18;17(24): 9519. doi: 10.3390/ ijerph17249519.	Excluded – Study did not focus on the experiences of autistics and COVID-19 or their parents
33730684* [a]	It took a Pandemic: Perspectives on Impact, Stress, and Telehealth from Caregivers of people with autism	White SW, Stoppelbein L, Scott H, Spain D.	Res Dev Disabil. 2021 Jun; 113:103938. doi: 10.1016/ j.ridd.2021.103938. Epub 2021 Mar 14.	Removed after the fourth step in PRISMA process
33892139[a]	Double Stranded RNA Drives Anti-viral Innate Immune Responses, Sickness Behavior and Cognitive Dysfunction Dependent on dsRNA length, IFNAR1 Expression and Age	McGarry N, Murray CL, Garvey S, Wilkinson A, Tortorelli L, Ryan L, Hayden L, Healy D, Griffin EW, Hennessy E, Arumugam M, Skelly DT, Mitchell KJ, Cunningham C.	Brain Behav Immun. 2021 Jul; 95:413–428. doi: 10.1016/ j.bbi.2021.04.016. Epub 2021 Apr 21.	Excluded – Study did not focus on the experiences of autistics and COVID-19 or their parents
34007506[a]	'This Is Not the Original Timeline': A Case Report of an Extended Dissociative Episode in a Healthy Young Male Accompanied with Severe Decline in Mental State	Tong G, Groom K, Ward L, Naeem M.	Case Rep Psychiatry. 2021 May 3;2021:6619579. doi: 10.1155/2021/6619579. eCollection 2021.	Excluded – Study did not focus on the experiences of autistics and COVID-19 or their parents

33389304[a]	Randomized Controlled Trial of a Video Gaming-Based Social Skills Program for Children on the Autism Spectrum	Beaumont R, Walker H, Weiss J, Sofronoff K.	J Autism Dev Disord. 2021 Oct;51(10):3637–3650. doi: 10.1007/s10803-020-04801-z. Epub 2021 Jan 3.	Excluded – Study did not focus on the experiences of autistics and COVID-19 or their parents
33486395[a]	How have youth with Autism Spectrum Disorder Managed Quarantine derived from COVID-19 Pandemic? An Approach to Families Perspectives	Mumbardó-Adam C, Barnet-López S, Balboni G.	Res Dev Disabil. 2021 Mar; 110:103860. doi: 10.1016/ j.ridd.2021.103860. Epub 2021 Jan 12.	Included in final analysis
34171493[a]	Parent Training Intervention for Autism Symptoms, Functional Emotional Development, and Parental Stress in Children with Autism Disorder: A Randomized Clinical Trial	Akhani A, Dehghani M, Gharraee B, Hakim Shooshtari M.	Asian J Psychiatr. 2021 Aug; 62:102735. doi: 10.1016/ j.ajp.2021.102735. Epub 2021 Jun 14.	Excluded – Study did not focus on the experiences of autistics and COVID-19 or their parents
34394851[b]	Transitioning ABA Services from in Clinic to Telehealth: Case Study of an Indian Organization's Response to COVID-19 Lockdown	Awasthi S, Aravamudhan S, Jagdish A, Joshi B, Mukherjee P, Kalkivaya R, Ali RS, Srivastava SN, Edasserykkudy S.	Behav Anal Pract. 2021 Aug 11;14(4):893–912. doi: 10.1007/s40617-021-00600-9. eCollection 2021 Dec.	Excluded – Study did not focus on the experiences of autistics and COVID-19 or their parents
31895812[a]	Effective/Cost Effective Interventions of Child Mental Health Problems in Low- and Middle-Income Countries (LAMIC): Systematic Review	Grande AJ, Ribeiro WS, Faustino C, de Miranda CT, Mcdaid D, Fry A, de Moraes SHM, de Oliveira SMDVL, de Farias JM, de Tarso Coelho Jardim P, King D, Silva V, Ziebold C, Evans-Lacko S.	Medicine (Baltimore). 2020 Jan;99(1):e18611. doi: 10.1097/ MD.0000000000018611.	Excluded – Study did not focus on the experiences of autistics and COVID-19 or their parents

(Continued)

PubMed ID	Article Title	Author(s)	Citation	Inclusion/Exclusion and Why
33845561[a]	Social Distancing and Social Interaction in Children with Autism Spectrum Disorder during the Covid-19 Pandemic: A Clinical Oxymoron	Trabacca A, Craig F.	Minerva Pediatr (Torino). 2021 Apr 12. doi: 10.23736/S2724-5276.21.06057-2. Online ahead of print.	Excluded – Opinion piece, commentary or letter to the editor
33465590* [a]	A Systematic Review of Technological Approaches for Autism Spectrum Disorder Assessment in Children: Implications for the COVID-19 Pandemic	Dahiya AV, DeLucia E, McDonnell CG, Scarpa A.	Res Dev Disabil. 2021 Feb; 109:103852. doi: 10.1016/j.ridd.2021.103852. Epub 2021 Jan 8.	Removed after the fourth step in PRISMA process
34827403[b]	A Multidisciplinary Telerehabilitation Approach for Supporting Social Interaction in Autism Spectrum Disorder Families: An Italian Digital Platform in Response to COVID-19	Vallefuoco E, Purpura G, Gison G, Bonifacio A, Tagliabue L, Broggi F, Scuccimarra G, Pepino A, Nacinovich R.	Brain Sci. 2021 Oct 25;11(11): 1404. doi: 10.3390/brainsci11111404.	Excluded – Study did not focus on the experiences of autistics and COVID-19 or their parents
34960514[b]	A New Socially Assistive Robot with Integrated Serious Games for Therapies with Children with Autism Spectrum Disorder and Down Syndrome: A Pilot Study	Panceri JAC, Freitas É, de Souza JC, da Luz Schreider S, Caldeira E, Bastos TF.	Sensors (Basel). 2021 Dec 16; 21(24):8414. doi: 10.3390/s21248414.	Excluded – Study did not focus on the experiences of autistics and COVID-19 or their parents

34986033[b]	Masking for School-Age Children with Epilepsy: We Do Have Consensus!	Fine AL, Wong-Kisiel LC, Nickels KC, Wirrell EC.	J Child Neurol. 2022 Feb;37(2): 127–132. doi: 10.1177/08830738211063684. Epub 2022 Jan 5.	Excluded – Study did not focus on the experiences of autistics and COVID-19 or their parents
33387743[a]	Changing Trends in Psychiatric Emergency Service Admissions during the COVID-19 Outbreak: Report from a Worldwide Epicentre	Gómez-Ramiro M, Fico G, Anmella G, Vázquez M, Sagué-Vilavella M, Hidalgo-Mazzei D, Pacchiarotti I, Garriga M, Murru A, Parellada E, Vieta E.	J Affect Disord. 2021 Mar 1; 282:26–32. doi: 10.1016/j.jad.2020.12.057. Epub 2020 Dec 27.	Excluded – Study did not focus on the experiences of autistics and COVID-19 or their parents
32905181[a]	Taking ACTion: 18 Simple Strategies for Supporting Children with Autism during the COVID-19 Pandemic	Tarbox CM, Silverman EA, Chastain AN, Little A, Bermudez TL, Tarbox J.	Behav Anal Pract. 2020 Sep 2; 14(4):1–29. doi: 10.1007/s40617-020-00448-5. Online ahead of print.	Excluded – Study did not focus on the experiences of autistics and COVID-19 or their parents
33285156[a]	Potential Health Benefits of Sustained Air Quality Improvements in New York City: A Simulation Based on Air Pollution Levels during the COVID-19 Shutdown	Perera F, Berberian A, Cooley D, Shenaut E, Olmstead H, Ross Z, Matte T.	Environ Res. 2021 Feb;193: 110555. doi: 10.1016/j.envres.2020.110555. Epub 2020 Dec 4.	Excluded – Study did not focus on the experiences of autistics and COVID-19 or their parents
32837696[a]	A Model of Support for Families of Children with Autism Living in the COVID-19 Lockdown: Lessons from Italy	Degli Espinosa F, Metko A, Raimondi M, Impenna M, Scognamiglio E.	Behav Anal Pract. 2020 Jun 2; 13(3):1–9. doi: 10.1007/s40617-020-00438-7. Online ahead of print.	Removed after the fourth step in PRISMA process

(Continued)

PubMed ID	Article Title	Author(s)	Citation	Inclusion/Exclusion and Why
33329142[a]	Sexual Health in Child and Adolescent Psychiatry: Multi-Site Implementation Through Synchronized Videoconferencing of an Educational Resource Using Standardized Patients	Drozdowicz L, Gordon E, Shapiro D, Jacobson S, Zalpuri I, Stewart C, Lewis AL, Robinson L, Myint MT, Daniolos P, Williamson ED, Pleak R, Graeff Martins AS, Gleason MM, Galanter CA, Miller S, Stubbe D, Martin A.	Front Psychiatry. 2020 Nov 17; 11:593101. doi: 10.3389/ fpsyt.2020.593101. eCollection 2020.	Excluded – Study did not focus on the experiences of autistics and COVID-19 or their parents
33988774[a]	Impact of COVID-19 on Community Participation and Mobility in Young Adults with Autism Spectrum Disorders	Pfeiffer B, Brusilovskiy E, Hallock T, Salzer M, Davidson AP, Slugg L, Feeley C.	J Autism Dev Disord. 2022 Apr;52(4):1553–1567. doi: 10.1007/s10803-021-05054-0. Epub 2021 May 14.	Included in final analysis
33369729[a]	The Effects of Transition to Technician-Delivered Telehealth ABA Treatment during the COVID-19 Crisis: A Preliminary Analysis	Pollard JS, LeBlanc LA, Griffin CA, Baker JM.	J Appl Behav Anal. 2021 Jan; 54(1):87–102. doi: 10.1002/ jaba.803. Epub 2020 Dec 28.	Excluded – Study did not focus on the experiences of autistics and COVID-19 or their parents
35367807[b]	Effect of Covid-19 Lockdown on Indian Children with Autism	Kaur R, Boobna T, Kallingal P.	Res Dev Disabil. 2022 Jun; 125:104230. doi: 10.1016/ j.ridd.2022.104230. Epub 2022 Mar 30.	Included in the post-survey analysis

34075809[a]	Food Insecurity in the Households of Children with Autism Spectrum Disorders and Intellectual Disabilities in the United States: Analysis of the National Survey of Children's Health Data 2016–2018	Karpur A, Vasudevan V, Lello A, Frazier TW, Shih A.	Autism. 2021 Nov;25(8): 2400–2411. doi: 10.1177/ 13623613211019159. Epub 2021 Jun 2.	Excluded – Study did not focus on the experiences of autistics and COVID-19 or their parents
35215136[b]	Pathogenic Infections during Pregnancy and the Consequences for Fetal Brain Development	Jash S, Sharma S.	Pathogens. 2022 Jan 31;11(2): 193. doi: 10.3390/ pathogens11020193.	Excluded – Study did not focus on the experiences of autistics and COVID-19 or their parents
35573336[b]	Autism Diagnostic Assessments with Children, Adolescents, and Adults Prior to and during the COVID-19 Pandemic: A Cross-Sectional Survey of Professionals	Spain D, Stewart GR, Mason D, Robinson J, Capp SJ, Gillan N, Ensum I, Happé F.	Front Psychiatry. 2022 Apr 28; 13:789449. doi: 10.3389/ fpsyt.2022.789449. eCollection 2022.	Excluded – Study did not focus on the experiences of autistics and COVID-19 or their parents
34609696[b]	Correction to: Predictors of Satisfaction with Autism Treatment Services during COVID-19	Ferguson EF, Jimenez-Muñoz M, Feerst H, Vernon TW.	J Autism Dev Disord. 2021 Oct 5:1. doi: 10.1007/s10803-021-05283-3. Online ahead of print.	Excluded – Study did not focus on the experiences of autistics and COVID-19 or their parents
34529837[b]	Loneliness and mental Health in Children and Adolescents with Pre-Existing Mental Health Problems: A rapid Systematic Review	Hards E, Loades ME, Higson-Sweeney N, Shafran R, Serafimova T, Brigden A, Reynolds S, Crawley E, Chatburn E, Linney C, McManus M, Borwick C.	Br J Clin Psychol. 2022 Jun; 61(2):313–334. doi: 10.1111/ bjc.12331. Epub 2021 Sep 16.	Excluded – Study did not focus on the experiences of autistics and COVID-19 or their parents

(*Continued*)

PubMed ID	Article Title	Author(s)	Citation	Inclusion/Exclusion and Why
32562437[a]	Making a Brochure about Coronavirus Disease (COVID-19) for Children with Autism Spectrum Disorder and their Family Members	Kawabe K, Hosokawa R, Nakachi K, Yoshino A, Horiuchi F, Ueno SI.	Psychiatry Clin Neurosci. 2020 Sep;74(9):498–499. doi: 10.1111/pcn.13090. Epub 2020 Jul 10.	Excluded – Opinion piece, commentary or letter to the editor
33879224[a]	Protocol for a Randomized pilot study (FIRST STEPS): Implementation of the Incredible Years-ASLD® program in Spanish Children with Autism and preterm Children with Communication and/or Socialization Difficulties	Valencia F, Urbiola E, Romero-González M, Navas I, Elías M, Garriz A, Ramírez A, Villalta L.	Trials. 2021 Apr 20;22(1):291. doi: 10.1186/s13063-021-05229-1.	Excluded – Study did not focus on the experiences of autistics and COVID-19 or their parents
33424652[a]	Moving Toward Telehealth Surveillance Services for Toddlers at Risk for Autism during the COVID-19 Pandemic	Conti E, Chericoni N, Costanzo V, Lasala R, Mancini A, Prosperi M, Tancredi R, Muratori F, Calderoni S, Apicella F.	Front Psychiatry. 2020 Nov 26; 11:565999. doi: 10.3389/fpsyt.2020.565999. eCollection 2020.	Excluded – Opinion piece, commentary or letter to the editor
33251819[a]	Teaching Small Talk: Increasing On-Topic Conversational Exchanges in College Students with Intellectual and Developmental Disabilities Using Remote Audio Coaching	Joseph B, Kearney KB, Brady MP, Downey A, Torres A.	Behav Modif. 2021 Mar;45(2): 251–271. doi: 10.1177/0145445520975174. Epub 2020 Nov 30.	Excluded – Study did not focus on the experiences of autistics and COVID-19 or their parents

33392143[a]	Excessive and Problematic Internet Use during the Coronavirus Disease 2019 School Closure: Comparison between Japanese Youth with and Without Autism Spectrum Disorder	Kawabe K, Hosokawa R, Nakachi K, Yoshino A, Horiuchi F, Ueno SI.	Front Public Health. 2020 Dec 17;8:609347. doi: 10.3389/fpubh.2020.609347. eCollection 2020.	Included in final analysis
34612710[b]	Evaluation of a Graduated Exposure Procedure to Teach Extended Mask Wearing in Various Settings to Children with Autism	Ertel HM, Wilder DA, Hodges AC.	Behav Modif. 2021 Oct 6: 1454455211049546. doi: 10.1177/01454455211049546. Online ahead of print.	Included in the post-survey analysis
35103038[b]	Career Adaptability of Parents of Children with Autism Spectrum Disorder	Ozdemir NK, Koç M.	Curr Psychol. 2022 Jan 27: 1–14. doi: 10.1007/s12144-021-02649-9. Online ahead of print.	Excluded – Study did not focus on the experiences of autistics and COVID-19 or their parents
35447501[b]	A Qualitative Examination of the Impact of the COVID-19 Pandemic on Children and Adolescents with Autism and their Parents	Stadheim J, Johns A, Mitchell M, Smith CJ, Braden BB, Matthews NL.	Res Dev Disabil. 2022 Jun; 125:104232. doi: 10.1016/j.ridd.2022.104232. Epub 2022 Apr 14.	Included in the post-survey analysis
33311431[a]	Three Cases of COVID-19 Pneumonia That Responded to Icosapent Ethyl Supportive Treatment	Suh W, Urits I, Viswanath O, Kaye AD, Patel H, Hall W, Eskander JP.	Am J Case Rep. 2020 Dec 14; 21:e928422. doi: 10.12659/AJCR.928422.	Excluded – Study did not focus on the experiences of autistics and COVID-19 or their parents

(*Continued*)

PubMed ID	Article Title	Author(s)	Citation	Inclusion/Exclusion and Why
34157904[a]	Behavioral Affect in Children with Autism Spectrum Disorder during School Closures Due to the COVID-19 Pandemic in Japan: A Case-Controlled Study	Hosokawa R, Kawabe K, Nakachi K, Yoshino A, Horiuchi F, Ueno SI.	Dev Neuropsychol. 2021 Jun 23:1–10. doi: 10.1080/87565641.2021.1939350. Online ahead of print.	Excluded – Case study
32841645[a]	Exceptionally High COVID-19 Viral Load and Very Long Duration of Shedding in a Young Pauci-Symptomatic Child with Autism Resident in an Italian Nursing Home	Grossi E, Terruzzi V.	J Infect. 2021 Feb;82(2): e29-e30. doi: 10.1016/j.jinf.2020.08.026. Epub 2020 Aug 22.	Excluded – Opinion piece, commentary or letter to the editor
33475040[a]	The Prospect of Autism in the Next Generation; the Need to Pay Attention to the COVID-19 Pandemic	Mohammadi MR, Zandifar A, Badrfam R.	World J Biol Psychiatry. 2021 Sep;22(7):557–558. doi: 10.1080/15622975.2021.1878390. Epub 2021 Apr 9.	Excluded – Opinion Piece, Commentary or letter to the editor
35275394[b]	Analysis of the Impact of COVID-19 on Youngsters with Autistic Spectrum Disorder	Salmerón-Medina M, Tàpia-Córcoles A, Palou-Artola E, Nicolau-Palou R, Calvo-Escalona R.	Rev Neurol. 2022 Mar 16; 74(6):181–188. doi: 10.33588/rn.7406.2021291.	Excluded – Article published in Spanish

34923834[b]	Home Direct-to-Consumer Telehealth Solutions for Children with Mental Health Disorders and the Impact of Covid-19	Norman S, Atabaki S, Atmore K, Biddle C, DiFazio M, Felten D, Fox E, Marschall D, Newman J, Robb A, Rowland C, Selekman R, Slovin A, Stein M, Strang J, Sable C.	Clin Child Psychol Psychiatry. 2022 Jan;27(1):244–258. doi: 10.1177/13591045211064134. Epub 2021 Dec 20.	Excluded – Study did not focus on the experiences of autistics and COVID-19 or their parents
34826776[b]	Risk and Protective Factors of Quality of life for Children with Autism Spectrum Disorder and their Families during the COVID-19 Lockdown. An Italian Study	Logrieco MG, Casula L, Ciuffreda GN, Novello RL, Spinelli M, Lionetti F, Nicolì I, Fasolo M, Giovanni V, Stefano V.	Res Dev Disabil. 2022 Jan; 120:104130. doi: 10.1016/j.ridd.2021.104130. Epub 2021 Nov 19.	Included in the post-survey analysis
33266429* [a]	Using Hybrid Telepractice for Supporting Parents of Children with ASD during the COVID-19 Lockdown: A Feasibility Study in Iran	Samadi SA, Bakhshalizadeh-Moradi S, Khandani F, Foladgar M, Poursaid-Mohammad M, McConkey R.	Brain Sci. 2020 Nov 22;10(11): 892. doi: 10.3390/brainsci10110892.	Removed after the fourth step in PRISMA process
33058519[a]	Debate: Remote Learning during COVID-19 for Children with high Functioning Autism Spectrum Disorder	Reicher D.	Child Adolesc Ment Health. 2020 Nov;25(4):263–264. doi: 10.1111/camh.12425. Epub 2020 Oct 15.	Excluded – Opinion piece, commentary or letter to the editor
33718591* [a]	Transition of a Judo Program from In-Person to Remote Delivery during COVID-19 for Youth with Autism Spectrum Disorder	Garcia JM, Cathy BS, Garcia AV, Shurack R, Brazendale K, Leahy N, Fukuda D, Lawrence S.	Adv Neurodev Disord. 2021; 5(2):227–232. doi: 10.1007/s41252-021-00198-7. Epub 2021 Mar 6.	Removed after the fourth step in PRISMA process

(*Continued*)

PubMed ID	Article Title	Author(s)	Citation	Inclusion/Exclusion and Why
35460894[b]	Autism Spectrum Disorder Screening during the COVID-19 Pandemic in a Large Primary Care Network	Wallis KE, Nekrasova E, Bennett AE, Fiks AG, Gerdes M, Jenssen BP, Miller JS, Shu D, Guthrie W.	Acad Pediatr. 2022 Apr 20: S1876-2859(22)00232-7. doi: 10.1016/ j.acap.2022.04.005. Online ahead of print.	Excluded – Study did not focus on the experiences of autistics and COVID-19 or their parents
35541570[b]	Impact of COVID-19 Pandemic-Associated Social Changes on Boys with Moderate to Severe Autism	Hannawi AP, Knight C, Grelotti DJ, Trauner DA.	Adv Neurodev Disord. 2022 May 6:1–5. doi: 10.1007/ s41252-022-00257-7. Online ahead of print.	Included in the post-survey analysis
34420427[b]	COVID-19 Risk: Adult Medicaid Beneficiaries with Autism, Intellectual Disability, and Mental Health Conditions	Schott W, Tao S, Shea L.	Autism. 2022 May;26(4): 975–987. doi: 10.1177/ 13623613211039662. Epub 2021 Aug 21.	Included in the post-survey analysis
35151216[b]	Investigating the Relationships between Resilience, Autism-Related Quantitative Traits, and Mental Health Outcomes among Adults during the COVID-19 Pandemic	Taylor SC, Smernoff ZL, Rajan M, Steeman S, Gehringer BN, Dow HC, Barzilay R, Rader DJ, Bucan M, Almasy L, Brodkin ES.	J Psychiatr Res. 2022 Apr;148: 250–257. doi: 10.1016/ j.jpsychires.2022.01.046. Epub 2022 Jan 29.	Excluded – Study did not focus on the experiences of autistics and COVID-19 or their parents
34405062[b]	Post Severe Acute Respiratory Syndrome Coronavirus 2 Infection Tremors in a Nonverbal Autistic Adolescent	Zariffeh A, Youssef AS, Rizvi F, Lew LQ.	Cureus. 2021 Jul 10;13(7): e16296. doi: 10.7759/ cureus.16296. eCollection 2021 Jul.	Excluded – Case study

35073995[b]	IDEAS: Individual Level Differential Expression Analysis for Single-Cell RNA-seq Data	Zhang M, Liu S, Miao Z, Han F, Gottardo R, Sun W.	Genome Biol. 2022 Jan 24; 23(1):33. doi: 10.1186/s13059-022-02605-1.	Excluded – Study did not focus on the experiences of autistics and COVID-19 or their parents
35133855[b]	Understanding Caregiver Satisfaction with a Telediagnostic Assessment of Autism Spectrum Disorder	Jones MK, Zellner MA, Hobson AN, Levin A, Roberts MY.	Am J Speech Lang Pathol. 2022 Mar 10;31(2):982–990. doi: 10.1044/2021_AJSLP-21-00139. Epub 2022 Feb 8.	Excluded – Study did not focus on the experiences of autistics and COVID-19 or their parents
32659945[a]	Effective Strategies for Managing COVID-19 Emergency Restrictions for Adults with Severe ASD in a Daycare Center in Italy	Brondino N, Damiani S, Politi P.	Brain Sci. 2020 Jul 9;10(7): 436. doi: 10.3390/brainsci10070436.	Removed after the fourth step in PRISMA process
34221461[b]	How the COVID-19 Pandemic Affects the Definition of a Condition?: A Commentary on the Diagnostic Process of Autism Spectrum Disorder	Rafiei M, Memari A.	Sultan Qaboos Univ Med J. 2021 May;21(2):e164-e165. doi: 10.18295/squmj.2021.21.02.002. Epub 2021 Jun 21.	Excluded – Opinion piece, commentary or letter to the editor
35426749[b]	Supporting Children on the Autism Spectrum as They Experience the Challenges of COVID-19	Obst B, Roesler M, Fato P, Goff C.	NASN Sch Nurse. 2022 Apr 15:1942602X221089047. doi: 10.1177/1942602X221089047. Online ahead of print.	Included in the post-survey analysis

(*Continued*)

PubMed ID	Article Title	Author(s)	Citation	Inclusion/Exclusion and Why
34193630[a]	WhatsApp-Based Physical Activity Intervention for Children with Autism Spectrum Disorder during the Novel Coronavirus (COVID-19) Pandemic: A Feasibility Trial	Esentürk OK, Yarımkaya E.	Adapt Phys Activ Q. 2021 Oct 1;38(4):569–584. doi: 10.1123/apaq.2020-0109. Epub 2021 Jun 30.	Removed after the fourth step in PRISMA process
34241594[b]	Impact of COVID-19 Lockdown on Sleep in Children with Autism Spectrum Disorders	Bruni O, Melegari MG, Breda M, Cedrone A, Finotti E, Malorgio E, Doria M, Ferri R.	J Clin Sleep Med. 2022 Jan 1; 18(1):137–143. doi: 10.5664/jcsm.9518.	Included in the post-survey analysis
34636703[b]	The Impact of the COVID-19 Pandemic on Children with Special Needs: A Descriptive Study	Mete Yesil A, Sencan B, Omercioglu E, Ozmert EN.	Clin Pediatr (Phila). 2022 Feb; 61(2):141–149. doi: 10.1177/00099228211050223. Epub 2021 Oct 12.	Excluded – Study did not focus on the experiences of autistics and COVID-19 or their parents
35422715[b]	Relationships between Mental Health, Emotion Regulation, and Meaning in Life of Frontline Nurses during the COVID-19 Outbreak	Chen S, Zhou W, Luo T, Huang L.	Front Psychiatry. 2022 Mar 29; 13:798406. doi: 10.3389/fpsyt.2022.798406. eCollection 2022.	Excluded – Study did not focus on the experiences of autistics and COVID-19 or their parents

35320253[b]	The role of Augmentative and Alternative Communication in Speech and Language Therapy: A Mini Review	Butt AK, Zubair R, Rathore FA.	J Pak Med Assoc. 2022 Mar; 72(3):581–584. doi: 10.47391/JPMA.22-023.	Excluded – Study did not focus on the experiences of autistics and COVID-19 or their parents
35572177[b]	The impact of the COVID-19 School Closures on Families with Children with Disabilities: A Qualitative Analysis	Lipkin M, Crepeau-Hobson F.	Psychol Sch. 2022 Apr 12: 10.1002/pits.22706. doi: 10.1002/pits.22706. Online ahead of print.	Excluded – Study did not focus on the experiences of autistics and COVID-19 or their parents
33271720[a]	Supporting Individuals with Autism Spectrum Disorder in Medical Settings during COVID-19	Goh TJ, Lim T, Foo M, Ong SKA, Aishworiya R, Nair T, Kang YQ, Agarwal PK, Sung M.	Asian J Psychiatr. 2020 Dec; 54:102441. doi: 10.1016/j.ajp.2020.102441. Epub 2020 Oct 9.	Excluded – Opinion piece, commentary or letter to the editor
34776249[b]	Anxiety and Depression in Parents of Children with Autism Spectrum Disorder during the First COVID-19 Lockdown: Report from the ELENA Cohort	Miniarikova E, Vernhet C, Peries M, Loubersac J, Picot MC, Munir K, Baghdadli A.	J Psychiatr Res. 2022 May; 149:344–351. doi: 10.1016/j.jpsychires.2021.11.022. Epub 2021 Nov 8.	Included in the post-survey analysis
35253243[b]	Life Under Lockdown for Children with Autism Spectrum Disorder: Insights from Families in South Africa	Adams SN, Seedat J, Neille J.	Child Care Health Dev. 2022 Mar 6. doi: 10.1111/cch.12996. Online ahead of print.	Excluded – Study did not focus on the experiences of autistics and COVID-19 or their parents

(*Continued*)

PubMed ID	Article Title	Author(s)	Citation	Inclusion/Exclusion and Why
34836713[b]	Parent Intentions to Vaccinate Children with Autism Spectrum Disorder Against COVID-19	Choi K, Becerra-Culqui T, Bhakta B, Bruxvoort K, Coleman KJ.	J Pediatr Nurs. 2022 Mar-Apr; 63:108–110. doi: 10.1016/j.pedn.2021.11.019. Epub 2021 Nov 24.	Included in the post-survey analysis
34951864[b]	Medical and Health-Related Misinformation on Social Media: Bibliometric Study of the Scientific Literature	Yeung AWK, Tosevska A, Klager E, Eibensteiner F, Tsagkaris C, Parvanov ED, Nawaz FA, Völkl-Kernstock S, Schaden E, Kletecka-Pulker M, Willschke H, Atanasov AG.	J Med Internet Res. 2022 Jan 25;24(1):e28152. doi: 10.2196/28152.	Excluded – Study did not focus on the experiences of autistics and COVID-19 or their parents
35234355[b]	Differential Effects of COVID-Related Lockdown on Sleep-Wake Rhythms in Adults with Autism Spectrum Disorder Compared to the General Population	Reynaud E, Pottelette J, Rabot J, Rolling J, Royant-Parola S, Hartley S, Coutelle R, Schröder CM.	Autism Res. 2022 May;15(5): 945–956. doi: 10.1002/aur.2692. Epub 2022 Mar 2.	Included in the post-survey analysis
35076831[b]	Impact of the COVID-19 Pandemic on Daily Life: Diverse Experiences for Autistic Adults	Maljaars J, Gijbels E, Evers K, Spain D, Rumball F, Happé F, Noens I.	J Autism Dev Disord. 2022 Jan 25:1–13. doi: 10.1007/s10803-022-05437-x. Online ahead of print.	Included in the post-survey analysis

35281673[b]	Teaching Adults with Neurodevelopmental Disabilities to Interact Successfully with Others in a Virtual Format	Callahan R, Kail B, Lerman DC, Johnson-Patagoc K, Whitcher D.	Behav Anal Pract. 2022 Mar 4: 1–17. doi: 10.1007/ s40617-022-00681-0. Online ahead of print.	Excluded – Study did not focus on the experiences of autistics and COVID-19 or their parents
32575062[a]	Supporting Children with Autism Spectrum Disorder in the Face of the COVID-19 Pandemic	Smile SC.	CMAJ. 2020 May 25;192(21): E587. doi: 10.1503/ cmaj.75399.	Excluded – Opinion piece, commentary or letter to the editor
35572181[b]	Exploring Telehealth during COVID for Assessing Autism Spectrum Disorder in a Diverse Sample	Stavropoulos KKM, Heyman M, Salinas G, Baker E, Blacher J.	Psychol Sch. 2022 Mar 25: 10.1002/pits.22672. doi: 10.1002/pits.22672. Online ahead of print.	Included in the post-survey analysis
34085153[a]	Transitioning to Telemedicine during COVID-19: Impact on Perceptions and Use of Telemedicine Procedures for the Diagnosis of Autism in Toddlers	Wagner L, Weitlauf AS, Hine J, Corona LL, Berman AF, Nicholson A, Allen W, Black M, Warren Z.	J Autism Dev Disord. 2022 May;52(5):2247–2257. doi: 10.1007/s10803-021-05112-7. Epub 2021 Jun 4.	Excluded – Study did not focus on the experiences of autistics and COVID-19 or their parents
35113328[b]	Brief Report: Covid Restrictions had Positive and Negative Impacts on Schooling for Students on the Autism Spectrum	Simpson K, Adams D.	J Autism Dev Disord. 2022 Feb 3:1–7. doi: 10.1007/ s10803-022-05451-z. Online ahead of print.	Included in the post-survey analysis
34081298[a]	Impact of School Closures due to COVID-19 on Children with Neurodevelopmental Disorders in Japan	Kawaoka N, Ohashi K, Fukuhara S, Miyachi T, Asai T, Imaeda M, Saitoh S.	J Autism Dev Disord. 2022 May;52(5):2149–2155. doi: 10.1007/s10803-021-05119-0. Epub 2021 Jun 3.	Excluded – Study did not focus on the experiences of autistics and COVID-19 or their parents

(*Continued*)

PubMed ID	Article Title	Author(s)	Citation	Inclusion/Exclusion and Why
33991289* [a]	Parental Views of Families of Children with Autism Spectrum Disorder and Developmental Disorders during the COVID-19 Pandemic	Meral BF.	J Autism Dev Disord. 2022 Apr;52(4):1712–1724. doi: 10.1007/s10803-021-05070-0. Epub 2021 May 15.	Removed after the fourth step in PRISMA process
35268354[b]	Parenting Children with Autism Spectrum Disorder during Crises: Differential Responses between the Financial and the COVID-19 Pandemic Crisis	Papanikolaou K, Ntre V, Gertsou IM, Tagkouli E, Tzavara C, Pehlivanidis A, Kolaitis G.	J Clin Med. 2022 Feb 25;11(5): 1264. doi: 10.3390/ jcm11051264.	Included in the post-survey analysis
35207180[b]	Multiple Aspects of Inappropriate Action of Renin-Angiotensin, Vasopressin, and Oxytocin Systems in Neuropsychiatric and Neurodegenerative Diseases	Szczepanska-Sadowska E, Wsol A, Cudnoch-Jedrzejewska A, Czarzasta K, Żera T.	J Clin Med. 2022 Feb 9;11(4): 908. doi: 10.3390/ jcm11040908.	Excluded – Study did not focus on the experiences of autistics and COVID-19 or their parents
35250672[b]	Maternal Immune Activation and Interleukin 17A in the Pathogenesis of Autistic Spectrum Disorder and Why It Matters in the COVID-19 Era	Carter M, Casey S, O'Keeffe GW, Gibson L, Gallagher L, Murray DM.	Front Psychiatry. 2022 Feb 17; 13:823096. doi: 10.3389/ fpsyt.2022.823096. eCollection 2022.	Excluded – Study did not focus on the experiences of autistics and COVID-19 or their parents

35124401[b]	Media use and Emotional Distress under COVID-19 Lockdown in a Clinical Sample Referred for Internalizing Disorders: A Swiss Adolescents' Perspective	Werling AM, Walitza S, Gerstenberg M, Grünblatt E, Drechsler R.	J Psychiatr Res. 2022 Mar; 147:313–323. doi: 10.1016/ j.jpsychires.2022.01.004. Epub 2022 Jan 5.	Excluded – Study did not focus on the experiences of autistics and COVID-19 or their parents
33635422[a]	Implications of Employment Changes Caused by COVID-19 on Mental Health and Work-Related Psychological Need Satisfaction of Autistic Employees: A Mixed-Methods Longitudinal Study	Goldfarb Y, Gal E, Golan O.	J Autism Dev Disord. 2022 Jan;52(1):89–102. doi: 10.1007/s10803-021-04902-3. Epub 2021 Feb 26.	Included in final analysis
34551900[b]	Feasibility and Parental Perception of home sleep Studies during COVID-19: A Tertiary Sleep centre Experience	Jones S, Hanwell R, Chowdhury T, Orgill J, van den Eshof K, Farquhar M, Joseph D, Gringras P, Trucco F.	Arch Dis Child. 2022 Feb; 107(2):189–191. doi: 10.1136/ archdischild-2021-322184. Epub 2021 Sep 22.	Excluded – Study did not focus on the experiences of autistics and COVID-19 or their parents
35053859[b]	The Psychological Impact of the COVID-19 Lockdown: A Comparison between Caregivers of Autistic and Non-Autistic Individuals in Italy	Fusar-Poli L, Martinez M, Surace T, Meo V, Patania F, Avanzato C, Signorelli MS, Aguglia E.	Brain Sci. 2022 Jan 15;12(1): 116. doi: 10.3390/ brainsci12010116.	Included in the post-survey analysis
35598429[b]	Fetal Neurodevelopmental Spatio-Temporal Dynamic Transcriptional Landscape of Maternal Insult-Induce Autism Spectrum Disorder Risk	Duan L, Yin H, Liu J, Wang W, Li J, Shen J, Liu L, Wang Z.	Biochem Biophys Res Commun. 2022 May 14;614: 183–190. doi: 10.1016/ j.bbrc.2022.05.040. Online ahead of print.	Excluded – Study did not focus on the experiences of autistics and COVID-19 or their parents

(Continued)

PubMed ID	Article Title	Author(s)	Citation	Inclusion/Exclusion and Why
35061560[b]	Cross-Platform Spread: Vaccine-Related Content, Sources, and Conspiracy Theories in YouTube videos Shared in early Twitter COVID-19 Conversations	Ginossar T, Cruickshank IJ, Zheleva E, Sulskis J, Berger-Wolf T.	Hum Vaccin Immunother. 2022 Dec 31;18(1):1–13. doi: 10.1080/ 21645515.2021.2003647. Epub 2022 Jan 21.	Excluded – Study did not focus on the experiences of autistics and COVID-19 or their parents
35579789[b]	Provider and Caregiver Satisfaction with Telehealth Evaluation of Autism Spectrum Disorder in Young Children during the COVID-19 Pandemic	Reisinger DL, Hines E, Raches C, Tang Q, James C, Keehn RM.	J Autism Dev Disord. 2022 May 17:1–15. doi: 10.1007/ s10803-022-05576-1. Online ahead of print.	Excluded – Study did not focus on the experiences of autistics and COVID-19 or their parents
35575840[b]	Incorporation of Telepsychiatry for Patients with Developmental Disorders into Routine Clinical Practice-A Survey of Specialty Clinics Adapting to Telepsychiatry during the COVID-19 Pandemic	Verma S, Vandana P, Soda T, Koth KA, Aguayo P, Shaffer RC, Hellings J, Muhle RA.	J Autism Dev Disord. 2022 May 16:1–5. doi: 10.1007/ s10803-022-05593-0. Online ahead of print.	Excluded – Study did not focus on the experiences of autistics and COVID-19 or their parents
33318802[a]	Sustained Compression Leading to Liner Pressure Ulcers Following Improper Surgical Mask Use in Autism Spectrum Disorder	Baba Y, Otani K, Sakai K, Kawaguchi R.	Acute Med Surg. 2020 Dec 10; 7(1):e604. doi: 10.1002/ ams2.604. eCollection 2020 Jan-Dec.	Excluded – Opinion piece, commentary or letter to the editor

32893073[a]	Convulsive Status Epilepticus as a Possible Symptom of COVID-19 in a Patient with Intellectual Disability and Autistic Spectrum Disorder	Peña-Salazar C, López Cuiña M, Chavarría V, Robles Olmo B.	Neurologia (Engl Ed). 2020 Nov-Dec;35(9):703–705. doi: 10.1016/j.nrl.2020.07.010. Epub 2020 Jul 31.	Excluded – Case study
35401276[b]	Effectiveness of Online-Delivered Project Impact for Children with ASD and Their Parents: A Pilot Study during the COVID-19 Pandemic	Li F, Wu D, Ren F, Shen L, Xue M, Yu J, Zhang L, Tang Y, Liu X, Tao M, Zhou L, Jiang L, Xu M, Li F.	Front Psychiatry. 2022 Mar 24; 13:806149. doi: 10.3389/fpsyt.2022.806149. eCollection 2022.	Excluded – Study did not focus on the experiences of autistics and COVID-19 or their parents
34483637[b]	Brief Report: Impact of the COVID-19 Pandemic on Asian American Families with Children with Developmental Disabilities	Dababnah S, Kim I, Wang Y, Reyes C.	J Dev Phys Disabil. 2022;34(3): 491–504. doi: 10.1007/s10882-021-09810-z. Epub 2021 Sep 1.	Excluded – Study did not focus on the experiences of autistics and COVID-19 or their parents
34121159[a]	The Digital Divide in Technologies for Autism: Feasibility Considerations for Low- and Middle-Income Countries	Kumm AJ, Viljoen M, de Vries PJ.	J Autism Dev Disord. 2022 May;52(5):2300–2313. doi: 10.1007/s10803-021-05084-8. Epub 2021 Jun 13.	Excluded – Study did not focus on the experiences of autistics and COVID-19 or their parents
35140635[b]	Group-Based Online Job Interview Training Program Using Virtual Robot for Individuals with Autism Spectrum Disorders	Kumazaki H, Yoshikawa Y, Muramatsu T, Haraguchi H, Fujisato H, Sakai K, Matsumoto Y, Ishiguro H, Sumiyoshi T, Mimura M.	Front Psychiatry. 2022 Jan 24; 12:704564. doi: 10.3389/fpsyt.2021.704564. eCollection 2021.	Excluded – Study did not focus on the experiences of autistics and COVID-19 or their parents

(Continued)

PubMed ID	Article Title	Author(s)	Citation	Inclusion/Exclusion and Why
32426099[a]	Maintaining Treatment Integrity in the Face of Crisis: A Treatment Selection Model for Transitioning Direct ABA Services to Telehealth	Rodriguez KA.	Behav Anal Pract. 2020 May 18;13(2):291–298. doi: 10.1007/s40617-020-00429-8. eCollection 2020 Jun.	Excluded – Opinion piece, commentary or letter to the editor
35410515[b]	Patient Satisfaction in Neurodevelopmental Pediatrics: In-Person vs Telemedicine	Kennelly AM, McIntyre B, Wood AC, Monteiro S, Voigt RG.	J Child Neurol. 2022 Mar; 37(3):181–185. doi: 10.1177/08830738221075451. Epub 2022 Apr 12.	Excluded – Study did not focus on the experiences of autistics and COVID-19 or their parents
35180544[b]	How Parents of Children with Autism Spectrum Disorder Experience the COVID-19 Pandemic: Perspectives and Insights on the New Normal	Bozkus-Genc G, Sani-Bozkurt S.	Res Dev Disabil. 2022 May; 124:104200. doi: 10.1016/j.ridd.2022.104200. Epub 2022 Feb 14.	Included in the post-survey analysis
34344221[b]	Special Education for Students with Autism during the COVID-19 Pandemic: 'Each day Brings new Challenges'	Hurwitz S, Garman-McClaine B, Carlock K.	Autism. 2022 May;26(4): 889–899. doi: 10.1177/13623613211035935. Epub 2021 Aug 3.	Included in the post-survey analysis
33730320[a]	Diagnostic Evaluations of Autism Spectrum Disorder during the COVID-19 Pandemic	Jang J, White SP, Esler AN, Kim SH, Klaiman C, Megerian JT, Morse A, Nadler C, Kanne SM.	J Autism Dev Disord. 2022 Feb;52(2):962–973. doi: 10.1007/s10803-021-04960-7. Epub 2021 Mar 17.	Excluded – Opinion piece, commentary or letter to the editor

35071743[b]	Human Services during the COVID Pandemic: Using Behavioral Safety Programs to Protect Human Services Workers and Students	Wine B, Doan T.	Adv Neurodev Disord. 2022 Jan 15:1–6. doi: 10.1007/s41252-021-00232-8. Online ahead of print.	Excluded – Study did not focus on the experiences of autistics and COVID-19 or their parents
34041682[a]	Brief Report: Impact of COVID-19 in Individuals with Autism Spectrum Disorders: Analysis of a National Private Claims Insurance Database	Karpur A, Vasudevan V, Shih A, Frazier T.	J Autism Dev Disord. 2022 May;52(5):2350–2356. doi: 10.1007/s10803-021-05100-x. Epub 2021 May 26.	Excluded – Study did not focus on the experiences of autistics and COVID-19 or their parents
34098745[a]	Pragmatic Adaptations of Telehealth-Delivered Caregiver Coaching for Children with Autism in the Context of COVID-19: Perspectives from the United States and South Africa	Franz L, Howard J, Viljoen M, Sikich L, Chandrasekhar T, Kollins SH, Lee L, Ndlovu M, Sabatos-DeVito M, Seris N, Shabalala N, Spanos M, de Vries PJ, Dawson G.	Autism. 2022 Jan;26(1): 270–275. doi: 10.1177/13623613211022585. Epub 2021 Jun 8.	Excluded – Opinion piece, commentary or letter to the editor
33606157* [a]	Characterizing Available Tools for Synchronous Virtual Assessment of Toddlers with Suspected Autism Spectrum Disorder: A Brief Report	Berger NI, Wainer AL, Kuhn J, Bearss K, Attar S, Carter AS, Ibanez LV, Ingersoll BR, Neiderman H, Scott S, Stone WL.	J Autism Dev Disord. 2022 Jan;52(1):423–434. doi: 10.1007/s10803-021-04911-2. Epub 2021 Feb 19.	Removed after the fourth step in PRISMA process
35103899[b]	Clinician Perspectives on Telehealth Assessment of Autism Spectrum Disorder during the COVID-19 Pandemic	Kryszak EM, Albright CM, Fell LA, Butter EM, Kuhlthau KA.	J Autism Dev Disord. 2022 Feb 1:1–16. doi: 10.1007/s10803-022-05435-z. Online ahead of print.	Excluded – Study did not focus on the experiences of autistics and COVID-19 or their parents

(*Continued*)

PubMed ID	Article Title	Author(s)	Citation	Inclusion/Exclusion and Why
33613859* [a]	Evaluating the Cool Versus Not Cool Procedure via Telehealth	Cihon JH, Ferguson JL, Lee M, Leaf JB, Leaf R, McEachin J.	Behav Anal Pract. 2021 Feb 12;15(1):260–268. doi: 10.1007/s40617-021-00553-z. eCollection 2022 Mar.	Removed after the fourth step in PRISMA process
35186135[b]	Children with Severe Disabilities: Adaptation, Virtual education, and Prospects. Experiences of three Peruvian Mothers, COVID-19 Context	Gamarra Choque PM, Rivera Arellano EG, Reynosa Navarro E, Méndez Vergaray J, Huayta-Franco YJ, Muñante Toledo MF.	J Med Life. 2022 Jan;15(1): 43–51. doi: 10.25122/jml-2021-0330.	Excluded – Study did not focus on the experiences of autistics and COVID-19 or their parents
35147653[b]	Sleep Behavior of Children with Autism Spectrum Disorder during the Covid-19 Pandemic: A Parent Survey	Scarselli V, Martucci M, Prono F, Giovannone F, Sogos C.	Clin Ter. 2022 Feb 7;173(1): 88–90. doi: 10.7417/CT.2022.2398.	Included in the post-survey analysis
34232419[b]	Development, Feasibility, and Acceptability of a Nationally Relevant Parent Training to Improve Service Access during the Transition to Adulthood for Youth with ASD	Taylor JL, Pezzimenti F, Burke MM, DaWalt LS, Lee CE, Rabideau C.	J Autism Dev Disord. 2022 Jun;52(6):2388–2399. doi: 10.1007/s10803-021-05128-z. Epub 2021 Jul 7.	Excluded – Study did not focus on the experiences of autistics and COVID-19 or their parents

35250452[b]	The Synaptic Gene Study: Design and Methodology to Identify Neurocognitive Markers in Phelan-McDermid Syndrome and NRXN1 Deletions	Cooke J, Molloy CJ, Cáceres ASJ, Dinneen T, Bourgeron T, Murphy D, Gallagher L, Loth E.	Front Neurosci. 2022 Feb 18; 16:806990. doi: 10.3389/ fnins.2022.806990. eCollection 2022.	Excluded – Study did not focus on the experiences of autistics and COVID-19 or their parents
35388450[b]	Parental Stress of Children with Autism Spectrum Disorder during the Coronavirus Pandemic (COVID-19): Experience from Serbia	Djuric-Zdravkovic A, Japundza-Milisavljevic M, Perovic D.	Fortschr Neurol Psychiatr. 2022 Apr 6. doi: 10.1055/ a-1743-2770. Online ahead of print.	Included in the post-survey analysis
35490214[b]	TV, Computer, Tablet and Smartphone Use and Autism Spectrum Disorder Risk in Early Childhood: A Nationally-Representative Study	Melchior M, Barry K, Cohen D, Plancoulaine S, Bernard JY, Milcent K, Gassama M, Gomajee R, Charles MA.	BMC Public Health. 2022 Apr 30;22(1):865. doi: 10.1186/ s12889-022-13296-5.	Excluded – Study did not focus on the experiences of autistics and COVID-19 or their parents
35255304[b]	Serum Glial Fibrillary Acidic Protein Is a Body Fluid Biomarker: A Valuable Prognostic for Neurological Disease – A Systematic Review	Heimfarth L, Passos FRS, Monteiro BS, Araújo AAS, Quintans Júnior LJ, Quintans JSS.	Int Immunopharmacol. 2022 Jun;107:108624. doi: 10.1016/ j.intimp.2022.108624. Epub 2022 Mar 4.	Excluded – Study did not focus on the experiences of autistics and COVID-19 or their parents
35162290[b]	Effects of the Early Phase of COVID-19 on the Autistic Community in Sweden: A Qualitative Multi-Informant Study Linking to ICF	Fridell A, Norrman HN, Girke L, Bölte S.	Int J Environ Res Public Health. 2022 Jan 24;19(3): 1268. doi: 10.3390/ ijerph19031268.	Excluded – Study did not focus on the experiences of autistics and COVID-19 or their parents

(*Continued*)

PubMed ID	Article Title	Author(s)	Citation	Inclusion/Exclusion and Why
35231721[b]	A Trial of Online Abracadabra Literacy Instruction with Supplementary Parent-Led Shared Book Reading for Children with Autism	Bailey B, Sellwood D, Rillotta F, Raghavendra P, Arciuli J.	Res Dev Disabil. 2022 May; 124:104198. doi: 10.1016/ j.ridd.2022.104198. Epub 2022 Feb 26.	Excluded – Study did not focus on the experiences of autistics and COVID-19 or their parents
34837543[b]	The Serbian Experience of Challenges of Parenting Children with Autism Spectrum Disorders during the COVID-19 Pandemic and the State of Emergency with Lockdown	Stankovic M, Stojanovic A, Jelena S, Stankovic M, Shih A, Stankovic S.	Eur Child Adolesc Psychiatry. 2022 Apr;31(4):693–698. doi: 10.1007/s00787-021-01917-0.	Included in the post-survey analysis
35319728[b]	Challenges of the COVID-19 Pandemic among Individuals with Autism Spectrum Disorder	Bitan DT, Krieger I, Weinstein O.	JAMA Psychiatry. 2022 May 1; 79(5):389–390. doi: 10.1001/ jamapsychiatry.2022.0237.	Excluded – Opinion piece, commentary or letter to the editor
35162512[b]	Social Skills Group Training for Students with Neurodevelopmental Disabilities in Senior High School-A Qualitative Multi-Perspective Study of Social Validity	Leifler E, Coco C, Fridell A, Borg A, Bölte S.	Int J Environ Res Public Health. 2022 Jan 28;19(3): 1487. doi: 10.3390/ ijerph19031487.	Excluded – Study did not focus on the experiences of autistics and COVID-19 or their parent

34929647[b]	A Paradoxical Psychological Impact of COVID-19 among a Sample of Italian Adults with High Functioning Autism Spectrum Disorder	Nisticò V, Gambini O, Pizzi L, Faggioli R, Priori A, Demartini B.	J Clin Neurosci. 2022 Jan;95: 27–30. doi: 10.1016/ j.jocn.2021.11.026. Epub 2021 Nov 29.	Included in the post-survey analysis
35369648[b]	Examining Clinicians' Concerns Delivering Telemental Health Interventions Directly to Autistic Individuals during COVID-19	Adams L, Adamo N, Hollocks MJ, Valmaggia L, Brewster A, Watson J, Krisson M, Simonoff E.	Res Autism Spectr Disord. 2022 Jun;94:101956. doi: 10.1016/ j.rasd.2022.101956. Epub 2022 Mar 29.	Excluded – Study did not focus on the experiences of autistics and COVID-19 or their parent
35564352[b]	The Effect of Sleep-Wake Routines on the Negative Emotional States and Aggressive Behaviors in Adults with Autism Spectrum Disorders (ASD) during the COVID-19 Outbreak	Levante A, Petrocchi S, Colombi C, Keller R, Narzisi A, Masi G, Lecciso F.	Int J Environ Res Public Health. 2022 Apr 19;19(9): 4957. doi: 10.3390/ ijerph19094957.	Included in the post-survey analysis
35184077[b]	Using Telehealth to Conduct Family-Centered, Movement Intervention Research in Children with Autism Spectrum Disorder during the COVID-19 Pandemic	Cleffi C, Su WC, Srinivasan S, Bhat A.	Pediatr Phys Ther. 2022 Apr 1; 34(2):246–251. doi: 10.1097/ PEP.0000000000000872.	Excluded – Study did not focus on the experiences of autistics and COVID-19 or their parent

(*Continued*)

PubMed ID	Article Title	Author(s)	Citation	Inclusion/Exclusion and Why
35268284[b]	Psychological Interventions for Children with Autism during the COVID-19 Pandemic through a Remote Behavioral Skills Training Program	Marino F, Chilà P, Failla C, Minutoli R, Vetrano N, Luraschi C, Carrozza C, Leonardi E, Busà M, Genovese S, Musotto R, Puglisi A, Arnao AA, Cardella G, Famà FI, Cusimano G, Vagni D, Martines P, Mendolia G, Tartarisco G, Cerasa A, Ruta L, Pioggia G.	J Clin Med. 2022 Feb 23;11(5): 1194. doi: 10.3390/ jcm11051194.	Excluded – Study did not focus on the experiences of autistics and COVID-19 or their parent
35409492[b]	Do Autistic Traits Correlate with Post-Traumatic Stress and Mood Spectrum Symptoms among Workers Complaining of Occupational Stress?	Dell'Osso L, Buselli R, Corsi M, Baldanzi S, Bertelloni CA, Marino R, Gravina D, Chiumiento M, Veltri A, Massimetti G, Caldi F, Perretta S, Foddis R, Guglielmi G, Cristaudo A, Carmassi C.	Int J Environ Res Public Health. 2022 Mar 23;19(7): 3809. doi: 10.3390/ ijerph19073809.	Excluded – Study did not focus on the experiences of autistics and COVID-19 or their parent

35083922[b]	The Impact of Early Stages of COVID-19 on the Mental Health of Autistic Adults in the United Kingdom: A Longitudinal Mixed-Methods Study	Bundy R, Mandy W, Crane L, Belcher H, Bourne L, Brede J, Hull L, Brinkert J, Cook J.	Autism. 2022 Jan 27: 13623613211065543. doi: 10.1177/ 13623613211065543. Online ahead of print.	Included in the post-survey analysis
35153690[b]	The Lonely Brain – Associations between Social Isolation and (Cerebro-) Vascular Disease from the Perspective of Social Neuroscience	Gronewold J, Engels M.	Front Integr Neurosci. 2022 Jan 28;16:729621. doi: 10.3389/fnint.2022.729621. eCollection 2022.	Excluded – Study did not focus on the experiences of autistics and COVID-19 or their parent
35464786[b]	Preliminary Practice Recommendations for Telehealth Direct Applied Behavior Analysis Services with Children with Autism	Araiba S, Čolić M.	J Behav Educ. 2022 Apr 16: 1–35. doi: 10.1007/ s10864-022-09473-6. Online ahead of print.	Excluded – Study did not focus on the experiences of autistics and COVID-19 or their parent
34626164[b]	Job loss Predicts Worsening Depressive Symptoms for Young Adults with Autism: A COVID-19 Natural Experiment	Taylor JL, Adams RE, Pezzimenti F, Zheng S, Bishop SL.	Autism Res. 2022 Jan;15(1): 93–102. doi: 10.1002/ aur.2621. Epub 2021 Oct 9.	Included in the post-survey analysis
35191848[b]	Digital Health Paradox: International Policy Perspectives to Address Increased Health Inequalities for People Living with Disabilities	van Kessel R, Hrzic R, O'Nuallain E, Weir E, Wong BLH, Anderson M, Baron-Cohen S, Mossialos E.	J Med Internet Res. 2022 Feb 22;24(2):e33819. doi: 10.2196/33819.	Excluded – Study did not focus on the experiences of autistics and COVID-19 or their parent
35572159[b]	Convulsive Status Epilepticus as a Possible Symptom of COVID-19 in a Patient with Intellectual Disability and Autistic Spectrum Disorder	Peña-Salazar C, López Cuiña M, Chavarría V, Robles Olmo B.	Neurologia. 2020 Nov-Dec; 35(9):703–705. doi: 10.1016/ j.nrl.2020.07.010. Epub 2020 Jul 31.	Excluded – Article published in Spanish

(*Continued*)

PubMed ID	Article Title	Author(s)	Citation	Inclusion/Exclusion and Why
35119331[b]	Acceptance of Telehealth Therapy to Replace In-Person Therapy for Autism Treatment during COVID-19 Pandemic: An Assessment of Patient Variables	Aranki J, Wright P, Pompa-Craven P, Lotfizadeh AD.	Telemed J E Health. 2022 Feb 3. doi: 10.1089/tmj.2021.0397. Online ahead of print.	Excluded – Study did not focus on the experiences of autistics and COVID-19 or their parent
35596024[b]	Brief Report: Feasibility of Delivering the Secret Agent Society Group Social Skills Program via Telehealth during COVID-19: A Pilot Exploration	Mootz CA, Lemelman A, Giordano J, Winter J, Beaumont R.	J Autism Dev Disord. 2022 May 20. doi: 10.1007/s10803-022-05591-2. Online ahead of print.	Excluded – Study did not focus on the experiences of autistics and COVID-19 or their parent
35064235[b]	Implications of Parental Stress on Worsening of Behavioral Problems in Children with Autism during COVID-19 Pandemic: 'The Spillover Hypothesis'	Eshraghi AA, Cavalcante L, Furar E, Alessandri M, Eshraghi RS, Armstrong FD, Mittal R.	Mol Psychiatry. 2022 Apr; 27(4):1869–1870. doi: 10.1038/s41380-021-01433-2. Epub 2022 Jan 21.	Included in the post-survey analysis
35064874[b]	Identifying Patient Characteristics to Understand Which Children May Receive Diagnostic Clarity in a Virtual Autism Spectrum Disorder Evaluation	Phelps RA, Sample E, Greene RK, Duvall SW.	J Autism Dev Disord. 2022 Jan 22:1–13. doi: 10.1007/s10803-022-05434-0. Online ahead of print.	Excluded – Study did not focus on the experiences of autistics and COVID-19 or their parent

35303712[b]	A Feasibility Trial for Virtual Administration of the Test of Gross Motor Development-3 for Children with Autism Spectrum Disorders during the COVID-19 Pandemic	Prieto LA, Meera B, Katz H, Columna L.	Adapt Phys Activ Q. 2022 Mar 18:1–10. doi: 10.1123/apaq.2021-0183. Online ahead of print.	Excluded – Study did not focus on the experiences of autistics and COVID-19 or their parent
35459604[b]	Food Insecurity in Households of Children with ASD in COVID-19 Pandemic: A Comparative Analysis with the Household Pulse Survey data using Stabilized Inverse Probability Treatment Weights	Karpur A, Vasudevan V, Frazier TW, Shih AJ.	Disabil Health J. 2022 Mar 26: 101323. doi: 10.1016/j.dhjo.2022.101323. Online ahead of print.	Excluded – Study did not focus on the experiences of autistics and COVID-19 or their parent
35385462[b]	Commentary on 'Using Telehealth to Conduct Family-Centered, Movement Intervention Research in Children with Autism Spectrum Disorder during the COVID-19 Pandemic'	Hall JB, Chole D, Wieberg L.	Pediatr Phys Ther. 2022 Apr 1; 34(2):252. doi: 10.1097/PEP.0000000000000890.	Excluded – Opinion piece, commentary or letter to the editor
35602995[b]	How Filipino Parents Home Educate Their Children with Autism during COVID-19 Period	Cahapay MB.	Int J Dev Disabil. 2020 Jun 22; 68(3):395–398. doi: 10.1080/20473869.2020.1780554. eCollection 2022.	Included in the post-survey analysis

Key:

*= Citations removed after step four of the Preferred Reporting Items for Systematic Reviews and Meta-Analysis (PRISMA) analysis process.

[a]= Citations retrieved from PubMed search conducted on 4 July 2021 and 27 May 2022, using the '(autis*[Title/Abstract]) AND (covid*[Title/Abstract])' search formula.

[b]= Citations retrieved from PubMed search conducted on 27 May 2022, using the '(autis*[Title/Abstract]) AND (covid*[Title/Abstract])' search formula.

APPENDIX 2 – THE ONLINE SURVEY

Question 1: Are you 18 years of age or over?
Potential responses:

- Yes
- No - Thanks for wanting to participate. However, this online survey is for adults. (This response ends the online survey).

Question 2: What is your gender identity?
Potential responses:

- Cis male
- Cis female
- Trans male
- Trans female
- Gender non-binary
- Other (please specify)

Question 3: How old are you?

- 18–25 years
- 26–35 years
- 36–45 years
- 46–55 years
- 56–65 years
- 65 + years

Question 4: What country do you live in?
Question 5: Do you have a formal autism diagnosis?
Potential responses:

- Yes
- No
- No, but I self-identify as autistic

Question 6: Have you experienced any restrictions that were related to the COVID-19 pandemic? For example, only being able to exercise with one other person, not travelling more than 5 kilometres (3.10 miles) from your home, or working from home arrangements?
Potential responses:

- Yes
- No

Question 7: What restrictions did you personally experience that were related to the COVID-19 pandemic?
Potential responses:

- Lockdown – could not leave home for 3 or more days
- Lockdown with ability to leave home for limited reasons
- Lockdown with limited freedom of movement (e.g. 1–5km travel only)
- Place of work changed to working from home all or part-time
- Social distancing
- Mask wearing in public places
- Other (please specify)

Question 8: What techniques and strategies did you use to cope with these restrictions? (You can choose more than one option)
Potential responses:

- I kept in contact with my friends
- I sought counselling or therapy
- I sought medical support
- I engaged in my hobbies to maintain focus and calm
- I exercised when I could
- I took a holiday
- I used non-prescription medication
- I used prescription medication
- Other (Please specify)

Question 9: Have you had one or more COVID-19 tests?
Potential responses:

- Yes
- No

Question 10: Have you had or do you have a diagnosis of COVID-19?
Potential responses:

- Yes
- No

Question 11: If diagnosed with COVID-19, did you access medical care?
Potential responses:

- I was hospitalised with COVID-19
- I cannot access medical care from where I live
- I do not know how to access medical care at the moment

- Yes – I was happy with my medical care
- Yes – but I was unhappy with my medical care
- No – I just self-isolated
- Other (Please specify)

Question 12: What are your opinions on the COVID-19 vaccine?
Potential responses:

- I am happy to be vaccinated
- I do not want to be vaccinated
- Comments

Question 13: Have you already had a COVID-19 vaccine?
Potential responses:

- Yes one dose
- Yes both doses
- Not yet, but I have made an appointment
- Not yet, but I want to
- No
- Other (Please specify)

Question 14: What are your reasons for wanting to be vaccinated against COVID-19? (You can select more than one option)
Potential responses:

- I want to help end the pandemic
- I want to protect myself against COVID-19
- I want to protect my family and/or friends against COVID-19
- I want to be exempt from pandemic-related restrictions
- I think the benefits outweigh the risks
- It is a requirement of my job
- Other (Please comment)

Question 15: What are your reasons for not wanting to be vaccinated?
Question 16: Are you currently raising a child or children on the autism spectrum?
Potential responses:

- Yes
- No

Question 17: Has your child on the autism spectrum tested for or been diagnosed with COVID-19?
Potential responses:

- Yes – they have been tested but did not have COVID-19
- Yes – they have been tested and were positive for COVID-19
- No – I wanted to get them tested but was unable to do so due to their distress
- No – I have not tried to get them tested
- Other (Please specify)

Question 18: Where did you seek help or look for information for your child on the autism spectrum after they were diagnosed with COVID-19 disease? (You can choose more than one option)
Potential responses:

- Medical doctors
- Family
- Friends
- Information about COVID-19 from the Internet
- Social supports (e.g. welfare agencies)
- More than one of the above
- Other (Please specify)

Question 19: What strategies are you teaching your child on the autism spectrum to protect themselves during the pandemic? (You can choose more than one option)
Potential responses:

- I am teaching my child to stay 1.5 metres (4.92 feet) from others
- I am teaching my child to wear a face mask
- I am teaching my child to wash their hands
- I am teaching my child to recognise the symptoms of COVID-19
- All/most of the above
- Other (Please specify)

Question 20: Are you intending to get your child on the autism spectrum vaccinated against COVID-19 when they are eligible?
Potential responses:

- Yes
- No

Question 21: Why do you intend to get your child/children on the autism spectrum vaccinated?
Potential responses:

- I want to help end the pandemic
- I want to protect child/children against COVID-19
- I want to protect my family and/or friends against COVID-19
- I want them to be exempt from pandemic-related restrictions
- Other (Please specify)

Question 22: Why are you not intending to get your child on the autism spectrum vaccinated?
Potential responses:

- I think the vaccine was developed too quickly
- I am concerned that the vaccine has side-effects
- My child has health issues that make the vaccine unsafe
- Other (Please specify)

Question 23: Is there anything else that you would like to say about the COVID-19 pandemic and being autistic and/or raising a child or children on the autism spectrum?
Free-text response.

Printed in the United States
by Baker & Taylor Publisher Services